Energy Almanac

52 Weekly Astrology Predictions & Holistic Resources For The Year Ahead

Copyright © 2023 Tam Veilleux. All rights reserved worldwide.

Thank you for buying an authorized edition of this book and for complying with copyright laws. You are respectfully entrusted to not reproduce, scan, distribute, transmit or record any part herein without prior permission, with the exception of brief quotations embodied in the critical reviews and certain other noncommercial uses permitted by copyright law. This publication contains material for educational purposes only. The author and publisher have made every effort to ensure that the information in the book was correct at press time and do not assume and hereby disclaim any liability to any party for any loss, damage, or disruption caused by errors and omissions.

Veilleux, Tam | Energy Almanac, 2023

Published by Luminous Moon Press, LLC
Edited by Michelle Schweitzer, Chelyn Consulting
Design by Carolyn Oakley, www.luminousmoon.com
Cover Art by Tam Veilleux, 2023

ISBN-13: 979-8-9874864-6-7

https://luminousmoon.com
https://choosebigchange.com

Luminous Moon Press, LLC, Choose Big Change, and its contributors are not doctors or lawyers of any kind. We do not diagnose or cure any disease, nor do we know the winning lottery numbers. We do not hold a license in any field except service to humanity. The contents herein are astrological opinions and holistic resources for you to accept or reject at will; this includes all nutritional suggestions. Using them does not replace or substitute available medical services, additional research, and good old-fashioned common sense. In fact, you are encouraged to verify anything we suggest with your doctor, psychic, or tarot deck. Do NOT use these suggestions if common sense tells you that it is not for you.

Ultimately, your spiritual, mental, emotional, and physical life, health and well-being are your responsibility. Tend to them well!

"I will love the light for it shows me the way,
yet I will endure the darkness because it shows me the stars."

–Og Mandino

FROM THE LEAD CREATOR OF
Energy Almanac

Well, dear reader, here we grow again! As you open the pages of our beloved Energy Almanac you are invited to let go of last year's crown of courage for facing change and pull on your workout clothes. This astrological year ahead requires big muscles for endurance and strength as you develop your own personal management style and bring order to the chaos that life sometimes is.

No worries, Little Pretzels—2024 shouldn't have you frightened. Built into the energy is a feeling of balance. Should you get thrown off kilter, your spiritual practices are always available to you. You worked them hard in 2023 through isolation, introspection and discovering new insights. For 2024 you'll use new tools, this time involving your own capacity to manage all the potentials in life. A front-of-mind theme for the year ahead includes grounding in and giving back. Grounding in what? Your spiritual practices (Neptune and Saturn in Pisces), an ongoing transformation (Pluto in Aquarius), new ways with prosperity (Uranus and Jupiter in Taurus), as well as a softer, gentler way of nurturing the world (Mars in Cancer). As joy comes into your life, share it outwardly. As gifts arrive, divide them up. Spare time? Walk with nature, join a prayer group, or practice yoga. Your dedication to building a solid foundation under a currently out-of-balance world is important.

Also of some urgency is the need to bone up on your leadership and management style. We are entering a year that requires each of us to step up in our own unique way (Chiron in Aries). Do identify your own personal wound in the area of leadership, strap on some courage and be the best YOU possible this year. As resources and our use of them shift, the world will need sovereigns who are willing to speak out for what is right and good for the group. Less passivity and more action on all of our parts should do the trick.

Collective change is here. And yes, you are one of the many pieces of the whole. Each decision to respond rather than react, to lead rather than blindly follow, to pray rather than try to control outcomes will create the softer, kinder world we all want to live in. Our article titled *Important Planetary Moves* will give you a general overview of some of the energies you'll experience in the year ahead.

The 2024 Energy Almanac is your guide for a year of well-balanced, properly planned use of time and money. It's a year for manifesting, too (read the numerology article). I'm sure you'll enjoy the latest collaboration of writers that gathered to share their expertise in a wide variety of topics. Beyond

Copyright © 2023 Tam Veilleux. All rights reserved worldwide.

that, I encourage you to lean into the weekly Human Design Gift & Shadow as you traverse the year ahead as a leader of the light.

Are you ready, Little Pretzel? Now is the time.

TAM VEILLEUX ♍

Artist/Alchemist/Astro-Junkie

PLEASE VISIT OUR ONLINE SHOP FOR THE HOLISTIC RESOURCES YOU NEED FOR 2024.

HTTPS://CHOOSEBIGCHANGE.COM

Copyright © 2023 Tam Veilleux. All rights reserved worldwide.

HOW TO USE YOUR

Energy Almanac

LEAVE IT IN A CONSPICUOUS LOCATION

- Be sure you leave the book where you'll see it often.
- Each week's astrology reads Monday through Sunday.

READ AND RE-READ

- Read the book all the way through one time, highlighting pieces of information that intrigue you or may be relevant according to date
- Read a second time with a notebook nearby—purposefully read and list information relevant to your life and profession
- Note key dates or themes i.e. moons, retrogrades, or choice points in your calendar system for easy reference
- Set a weekly reminder on your phone so you never forget to check the astrological prediction for the week ahead

Copyright © 2023 Tam Veilleux. All rights reserved worldwide.

How the Planets Play

PLANETS

Recall, if you will, the Roman myths we learned. Think of the ten planets as actors from those tales. Each planet is named after a character in a story with its own personality and traits. For example, in mythology, Saturn was the god of time and taught agriculture to his people. Saturn rules time, karma, discipline, and responsibility.

ZODIAC SIGNS

Consider the twelve zodiac signs as pieces of clothing that the planets might wear for a period of time. Each sign has specific qualities, traits, strengths, weaknesses, and general attitudes toward life. When a planet is traversing in any specific sign, its personality will be affected by the qualities of the sign. Example: The zodiac sign of Virgo is known for being analytical, health-oriented, mentally astute, detailed, preachy, overwhelmed, self-critical, and uptight.

ASTROLOGICAL HOUSES

The twelve houses of astrology represent where the character of the story will be. It's the stage or scene they will act in. The houses range from internal areas such as values, wishes and goals, shadow work, or identity to more external and tangible areas such as children, money, religion, and career. As a planet moves through a house, that area of life will feel the pressure of said planet.

ASPECTS

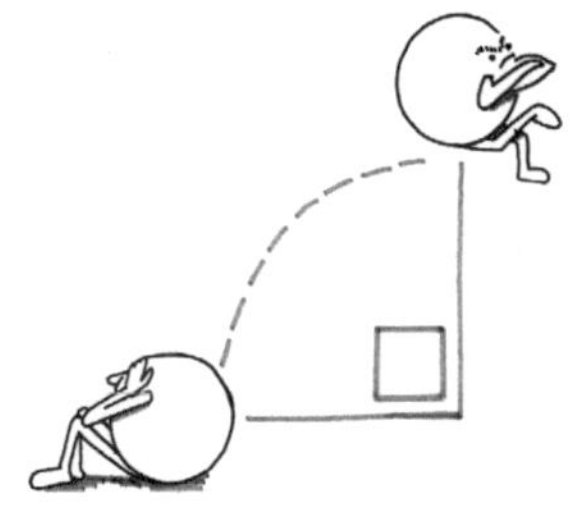

Aspects speak to how exactly the characters will play together based on where they are located. Maybe they'll be kind to one another (conjunct), or maybe someone will take their ball and go home (opposition). Some aspects create ease (conjunct, sextile) while others create discord (square, Grand Cross) and tension. Aspects are neither good nor bad. They simply show the relationship between planets.

♡ Love the Energy Almanac? Tag us on social media: @TheEnergyAlmanac ♡

Copyright © 2023 Tam Veilleux. All rights reserved worldwide.

Planets

Think of the ten planets as actors. Each planet is a character in a story, each with its own personality and traits indicating what the character/planet must do.

SUN 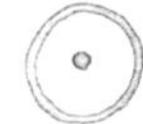

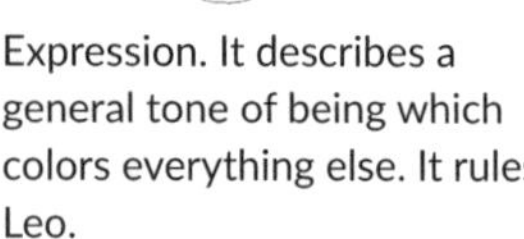

Expression. It describes a general tone of being which colors everything else. It rules Leo.

MOON

Emotion. It represents our feelings and emotions, the receptivity, intuition, imagination, and basic feeling tone of a person. It also affects our sense of rhythm and time. It rules Cancer.

MERCURY 

Communication. It represents reason, common sense, analyzing, data collection and the process of learning and skills. It rules Gemini and Virgo.

VENUS 

Relations. It gives us a sense of pleasure, aesthetic awareness, love of harmony, sociability, partnership, and eroticism. It rules Libra and Taurus.

MARS

Action. It represents the energy and drive of a person; courage, determination, the freedom of spontaneous impulse. It also describes the readiness for action, the way one goes about doing things, and simple aggression. It rules Aries.

JUPITER 

Expansion. It represents the search for individual meaning and purpose, optimism, hope, and a sense of justice, along with faith, a basic philosophy of life, wealth, religion, spiritual growth. It rules Sagittarius.

SATURN

Limitation. It shows how we experience "reality," where we meet with resistance and discover our limitations, moral convictions, and structure. It lends qualities like earnestness, caution, and reserve. It rules Capricorn.

URANUS 

Revelation. It represents intuition, originality, independence, and an openness for all that is new, unknown, and unusual. It creates a shift in thinking. It rules Aquarius.

NEPTUNE 

Compassion. It represents the mysterious and supersensory, mystical experience, and is creative, intuitive, and imaginative. Watch for deception, illusion, and false appearances as well as escapism in all its forms. It rules Pisces.

PLUTO 

Regeneration. It represents power. It is how we meet the demonic and magical. Pluto addresses our radical change via death and rebirth; it is passionate, intense, and global. It rules Scorpio.

THIS INFORMATION IS NOW AVAILABLE AS AN ONLINE CLASS.
Go to www.choosebigchange.com search SYNC+Thrive

Copyright © 2023 Tam Veilleux. All rights reserved worldwide.

Zodiac Signs

Each zodiac sign carries specific tendencies and traits. Think of them as a costume that the planet pulls on as it progresses through the sign. The costume indicates how the planet will behave.

ARIES ♈

MARCH 21-APRIL 19

Fire. Ruled by Mars. Brave, Direct, Fearless, Bold, Independent, Natural born leaders. Aggressive, Pushy, Selfish, Inconsistent. Think: Football uniform

TAURUS ♉

APRIL 20-MAY 20

Earth. Ruled by Venus. Steady, Loyal, Tenacious, Trustworthy, Patient. Resistant to change, Stubborn, Materialistic, Indulgent. Think: Denim overalls

GEMINI ♊

MAY 21-JUNE 20

Air. Ruled by Mercury. Intelligent, Adaptable, Communicative, Agile, Socially connected. Talkative, Superficial, Cunning, Exaggerating. Think: Color-blocked shirt

CANCER ♋

JUNE 21-JULY 22

Water. Ruled by the Moon. Nurturing, Supportive, Compassionate, Loving, Healing. Dependent, Indirect, Moody, Passive-aggressive, Holds on too long. Think: Fluffy bathrobe

LEO ♌

JULY 23-AUG 22

Fire. Ruled by the Sun. Brave, Generous, Charismatic, Fun, Playful, Warm, Protective. Egotistical, Controlling, Drama King/Queen, Dominating, Shows off. Think: Sundress and microphone

VIRGO ♍

AUG 23-SEPT 22

Earth. Ruled by Mercury. Modest, Orderly, Practical, Down-to-earth, Logical, Altruistic, Organized. Obsessive, Perfectionist, Critical, Overly analytical. Think: Medical lab coat

LIBRA ♎

SEPT 23-OCT 22

Air. Ruled by Venus. Charming, Diplomatic, Polished, Sweet-natured, Social. Indecisive, Superficial, Out of balance, Gullible, People pleasing. Think: Sequined dress, diamonds, and a scale

SCORPIO ♏

OCT 23-NOV 21

Water. Ruled by Mars and Pluto. Passionate, Driven, Perceptive, Determined, Sacrificing, Emotional Depth. Vindictive, Jealous, Paranoid, Destructive, Possessive, Passive-aggressive. Think: Black hoodie

SAGITTARIUS ♐

NOV 22-DEC 21

Fire. Ruled by Jupiter. Ambitious, Lucky, Optimistic, Enthusiastic, Open-minded, Moral. Restless, Blunt, Irresponsible, Tactless, Lazy, Overly indulgent. Think: Logo T-shirt and backpack

CAPRICORN ♑

DEC 22-JAN 19

Earth. Ruled by Saturn. Driven, Disciplined, Responsible, Persistent, Business-minded. Pessimistic, Greedy, Cynical, Rigid, Miserly, Ruthless. Think: Three-piece suit

AQUARIUS ♒

JAN 20-FEB 18

Air. Ruled by Saturn and Uranus. Intelligent, Inventive, Humanitarian, Friendly, Reformative. Emotionally detached, Impersonal, Scattered, Non-committal. Think: Astronaut outfit

PISCES ♓

FEB 19-MARCH 20

Water. Ruled by Neptune. Mystical, Intuitive, Compassionate, Romantic, Creative, Sensitive. Escapist, Victims, Codependent, Unrealistic, Submissive, Dependent. Think: Artists' smock

♡ Love the Energy Almanac? Tag us on social media: @TheEnergyAlmanac ♡

Copyright © 2023 Tam Veilleux. All rights reserved worldwide.

Copyright © 2023 Tam Veilleux. All rights reserved worldwide.

2024 Energy Sketch

JAN OPPORTUNITIES ARE WELL-TIMED & SOLID

FEB

MAR ECLIPSE SEASON

APR

MAY E-X-P-A-N-D-I-N-G IDEAS AROUND LEARNING

JUNE

JULY RETROGRADE SEASON BEGINS

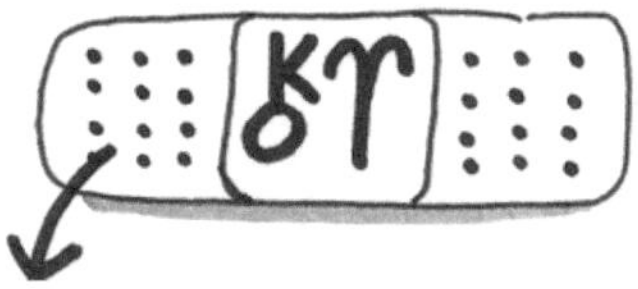

AUG FEELING INTO SOCIETAL SHIFTS

SEPT

OCT ECLIPSE SEASON

NOV 3 GRAND TRINES → Progress

DEC URGENT NEED FOR PRAGMATISM & SERVICE TO OTHERS

2025

2024 = 8

AS ABOVE, SO BELOW

IN OUT

FORM

STRUCTURE

MANAGEMENT & MANIFESTATION

balance

LEADERSHIP

ABUNDANCE

HEAL YOUR LEADERSHIP WOUND

Energy Almanac 2024 EDITION

Copyright © 2023 Tam Veilleux. All rights reserved worldwide.

Important Planetary Moves

The large outer planets play an interesting and effective role in the psyches of the masses. Their influence on human behavior can often be witnessed in the evening news. In order to understand what the mundane world might experience due to planetary placements we must look to Pluto, Uranus, Neptune, Jupiter, and Saturn individually. Each of these planets have their own role depending on which zodiac costume they are wearing. Let's take a look at the characters for the year ahead.

Here is your first reminder to grab your bonus Retrograde Report which you can find on the bonus page. Collect all the bonuses at:* ***www.choosebigchange.com/pages/bonus24

PLUTO IN CAPRICORN AND AQUARIUS

Pluto will move from Capricorn to Aquarius and back to Capricorn due to retrograde before ending in Aquarius in December.

Pluto in Capricorn in its final degree of the sign represents the complete regeneration of institutions as we know them. Pluto's work is to expose what isn't working and knock it out of place so that something new can be built. The three-piece suit of Capricorn represents all the imposing traditional systems that have been in place for hundreds of years. Look around. Is government, banking, healthcare, education the same as it was ten years ago? No. And thank Heavens so. Pluto has done big work.

Pluto in Aquarius in its earliest degrees brings about the foreshadowing of the rebuilding of society. Pluto, if you think of him as the Tasmanian Devil, will bring down old ideas about how we care for the group and force society to find new ways of handling all of those in the margins. Since Aquarius is futuristic and is the manager of "invisible waves," it's likely that there will be some new ways of using technology for the better. Down with using technology for spying on others, up with technology that heals us. (Watch for the impact of AI on our world—we will be grappling with the ethics and morality of this technology.)

NEPTUNE IN PISCES

The placement of Neptune in Pisces heightens your spirituality, intuition, and creativity as well as your compassion. It's a season for amplifying your inner world with ritual, prayer, sound, journaling, and impassioned intention setting. Make listening to the voices within part of your daily practice and put your faith in the unseen, knowing miracles are available to you if you will have them. Pisces is represented by the flowing artists' smock. He is a dreamer and visionary full of love for humanity. Your imagination will be heightened so be mindful of not escaping into your dreamworld full time. Put boots on the ground with a plan in hand to keep yourself moving toward the vision you created. A tendency toward forms of addiction and foggy thinking are the shadow sides to be concerned with.

URANUS IN TAURUS

The planet of revelation, Uranus, will be in the steady sign of Taurus for the entire year. Change is in the air when this planet spends its time in the area of our resources and self-worth. Its main desire is to shift slow-moving society into new ways with money and value systems. Uranus is future oriented and digital; Taurus is sensual and slow to change. The battle is on and the resistance is real, but Uranus will ultimately have his way. Watch the financial world globally as well as closer to home. Mind your resources carefully until things settle and, in the meantime, do some personal work developing your worthiness.

Copyright © 2023 Tam Veilleux. All rights reserved worldwide.

SATURN IN PISCES

The "cosmic thumb" of the cosmos, Saturn, is the bringer of lessons. He expects discipline, integrity, and responsibility as well as a tight grip on timing. When wearing the flowing artists' smock of Pisces, Saturn offers us a taste of "magical realism," the opportunity to dream it and then put a foundation under it. While Saturn creates limits, the big dreamer Pisces is limitless in its expectations. This transit involves dissolving boundaries (self-imposed or otherwise) and rethinking habits while developing spiritual practices. It's time to take your spirituality seriously, Little Pretzel.

JUPITER IN TAURUS

If Saturn reminds you of Grandpa, think of Jupiter as the "cosmic cheerleader." The nearly exact opposite energy of his societal counterpart, Jupiter brings hope, optimism, big-thinking, a sense of adventure, opportunity and abundance. He spent half of 2023 wearing the denim overalls of Taurus, giving us great reason to smile about our money and self-worth. He's comfy in the Taurus garb and will stay here expanding resources and providing new opportunities for you through May when he changes costumes.

When Jupiter is wearing the students' color-blocked button-down shirt with a pocket protector in place, you know that curiosity is high. This set-up is designed to help society develop new ideas around education and learning. It's also a highly social time and the urge to gather may be present, too. If you haven't already, do buy yourself a bunch of notebooks as Gemini loves communication. As your questions arise and answers follow, capture all of it.

GRAND TRINES & T-SQUARES

2024 is loaded with planetary action. Well, aren't they all?! But in particular for the year ahead are two T-Squares and three Grand Trines. The T-Squares are big energy that will force a shift or at the very least a need to seek solid ground. There is one happening in earth signs and two happening in water signs. We speak about them in more detail in the context of which they occur.

The Grand Trines are when three planets in the same element form a perfect equilateral triangle. As transits go, Grand Trines are relatively easy to handle and generally auspicious in nature. We will review the elements and opportunities of the trines as they occur later in this year's content.

VISIT OUR ONLINE STORE FOR JOURNALS THAT SUPPORT YOUR 2024 JOURNEY

HTTPS://CHOOSEBIGCHANGE.COM

Copyright © 2023 Tam Veilleux. All rights reserved worldwide.

Marvelous Moon Work

Every time I catch a glimpse of the Moon hanging in the sky, I literally gasp out loud. She could be a sliver, almost full, or half dark, in the middle of the night, at the cusp of the day, or in broad sunlight. Her beauty is always striking and it moves my soul.

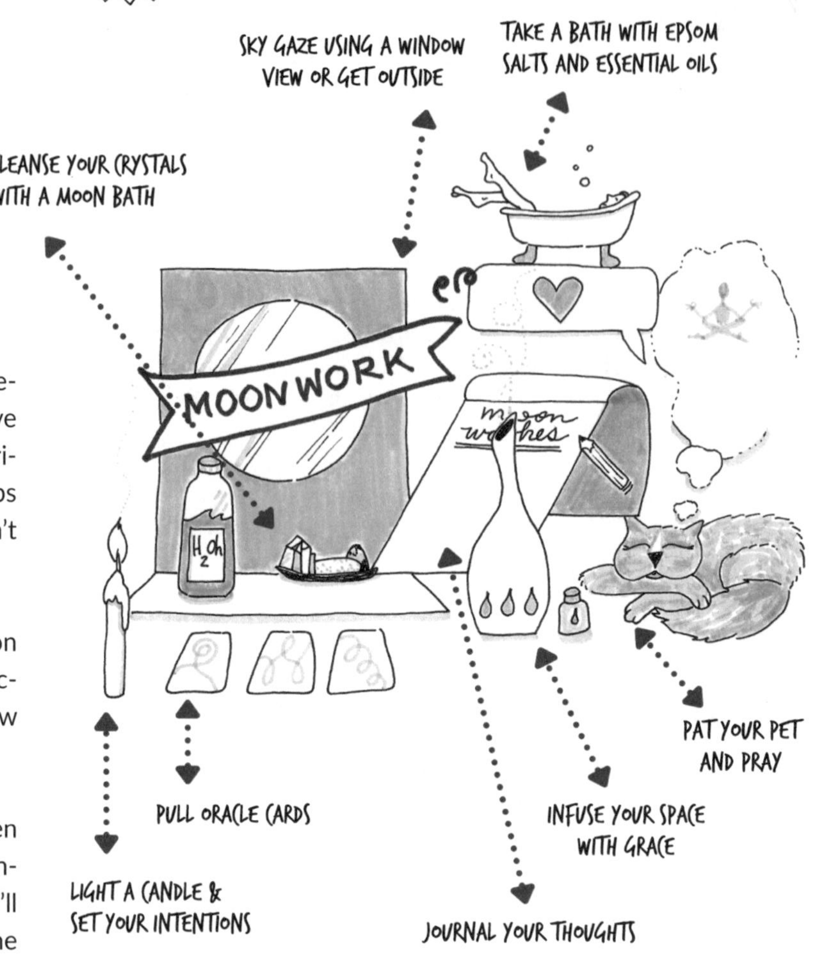

Luna is special. She's not like the other celestial bodies in our solar system. We have an intimate relationship, one based in spirituality and emotion. Without her, the ebbs and flows of nature, and our lives, wouldn't be possible.

Honoring our connection with the Moon twice monthly is a powerful spiritual practice. And it doesn't take more than a few mindful actions and contemplation.

Each new and full moon article is written specifically to reflect all the astrological energies swirling about at that given time. You'll find an affirmation to mentally reinforce the theme of that particular moon. As well as three pieces of monthly moonwork to embody it.

Approach these writings with a curious mind and an open heart. They were lovingly curated with the intention to support your highest good and spiritual wellbeing. If you're reading the Energy Almanac this year, these messages were destined to find you.

SARA RAE, Libra, is the author, podcaster, and manifesting coach behind *Spiritually Inspired.* While she specializes in astrology, meditation, and crystal reiki, she dabbles in all things metaphysical. From reading tarot cards, to practicing yoga, to channeling, to sound healing and chakra work, there are very few new age topics she isn't familiar with. There's nothing she's more passionate about than sharing the esoteric knowledge she discovers with other modern mystics all over the world. Find her podcast titled *Spiritually Inspired* wherever you get your podcasts.

www.SpirituallyInspired.co | IG @sararae.coach

Copyright © 2023 Tam Veilleux. All rights reserved worldwide.

A Note About Eclipses

Each year, at least two of the New and Full Moons are also a Solar or Lunar Eclipse. These dynamic events take place when the Sun, Earth, and Moon align so that the New Moon will cover the face of the Sun from the earth's perspective, creating the Solar Eclipse, or the Earth will block the Sun's light from reaching the Full Moon, bringing the Lunar Eclipse.

Eclipses are a function of the lunar nodes. The North Node (what we need more of) is in Aries and is involved with the Solar Eclipses in 2024. The South Node (what we need to release) is in Libra. We are learning how to express our true selves in our relationships without compromising our authenticity

An eclipse indicates a major change will arrive. It has a 6-month influence and can be felt as far as six weeks before it occurs. The Solar Eclipse is about identity and marks a change in an outer world circumstance; the Lunar Eclipse is about feelings and marks a change in relationships. Avoid beginning new ventures on or during the week before and after an eclipse.

All times throughout the Almanac are Eastern Time Zone.

MARCH 25
FULL MOON PENUMBRAL LUNAR ECLIPSE AT 5° LIBRA

APRIL 8
NEW MOON TOTAL SOLAR ECLIPSE AT 19° ARIES

SEPTEMBER 17
SUPER FULL MOON LUNAR ECLIPSE AT 25° PISCES

OCTOBER 2
NEW MOON SOLAR ECLIPSE AT 10° LIBRA

OCTOBER 17
FULL MOON PENUMBRAL ECLIPSE AT 24° ARIES

Copyright © 2023 Tam Veilleux. All rights reserved worldwide.

The Lunar Nodes

The two Lunar Nodes are a specific moving point in space where the Sun and Moon's orbital paths around the Earth intersect. Unlike the planets, the Moon's nodes move in a clockwise direction—Taurus toward Aries, for example—around the zodiac. The north node represents the way forward or karmic destiny; it is considered as Jupiter, a point where benefits are found. It represents a positive evolutionary direction, what we need to learn, our cosmic mission so to speak. The South Node is considered as Saturn, or karmic history and lessons, a point of constriction. It represents old instincts that must be transformed. The 2024 nodes are noted below. These muted energies will be working in the subconscious of everyone.

NORTH NODE

ARIES (NORTH)
JULY 18 – FEBRUARY 28, 2025

It's time to boldly step forth and lead. Bolster yourself for dynamic movement and initiating new ways of being. We will witness and partake in passionate leadership. Bravery may be required and be mindful of being overly zealous.

What is the energy of bold action taking?
How can I demonstrate dynamic leadership?

SOUTH NODE

LIBRA (SOUTH)
JULY 18 – FEBRUARY 28, 2025

This is no time for indecisiveness or passivity. With Libra in the south node, we can expect the need to employ more balance and fair outcomes. No more sitting quietly on the sidelines, it's time to get off the sofa and take part in the change the world needs. Someone is counting on you, be reliable!

What would it be like to make a decision and go after it enthusiastically?
How can I be more authoritative in my decision making?

YOU CAN FIND AMAZING BONUS CONTENT AT:
WWW.CHOOSEBIGCHANGE.COM/PAGES/BONUS24

Copyright © 2023 Tam Veilleux. All rights reserved worldwide.

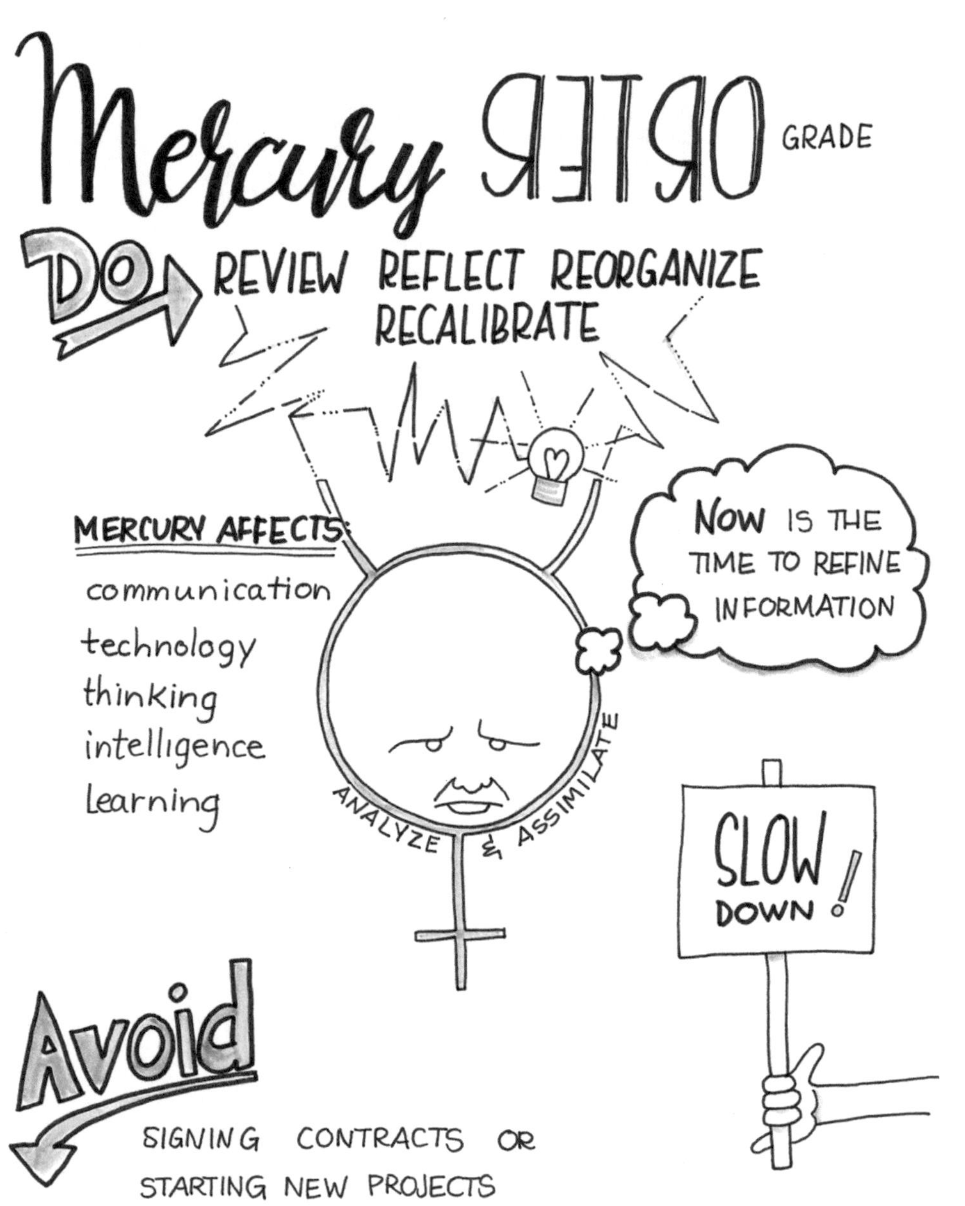

MERCURY RETROGRADE IN ARIES APRIL 1 – 24

- Revise your action plan. Review your leadership style. Recognize the level of courage you're employing.

MERCURY RETROGRADE IN VIRGO AUGUST 5 – 15

- Reorganize what needs it. Review your health. Redirect critical thinking.

MERCURY RETROGRADE IN LEO AUGUST 16 – 27

- Revisit what you're passionate about. Review the level of drama you're emitting. Reengage with creative endeavors.

MERCURY RETROGRADE IN SAGITTARIUS NOVEMBER 26 – DECEMBER 14

- Rethink your beliefs. Reprioritize adventure. Research new philosophies.

GET YOUR BONUS RETROGRADE REPORT BY GOING TO:

WWW.CHOOSEBIGCHANGE.COM/PAGES/BONUS24

Copyright © 2023 Tam Veilleux. All rights reserved worldwide.

Numerology

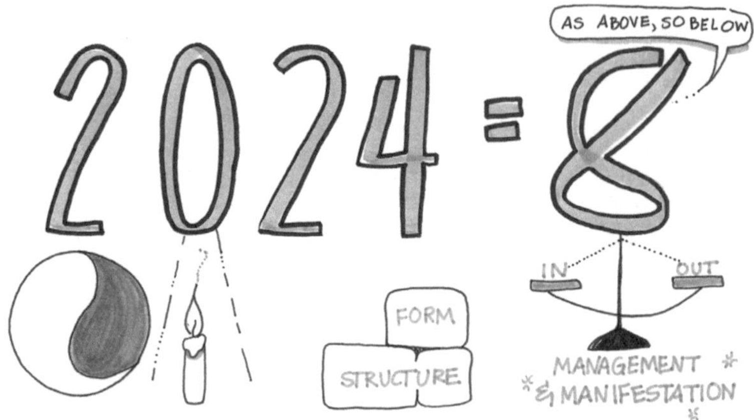

Numerology has roots in both Eastern and Western traditions and has been practiced for thousands of years in many cultures. In ancient times, numbers were thought to have a powerful influence and significance. The practice was used for divination and predictions about the future. In the modern age, people have incorporated numerology into their daily lives, using it to gain insight into their personal relationships, select names for their children, and to decide the best times to make important decisions.

Numerology once was considered a respectable academic subject as well as a science. In more modern times, it has been taught more as a pseudo-science and shunned by many. Excitingly, numerology is coming back into the public awareness and is growing in popularity. In the Energy Almanac we will focus on the energies for the overall year as well as each individual month. Being aware and understanding the energies can help us navigate and plan our daily lives around and with these energies. You can also dig deeper and plan around your own numerology energies working with your personal year and month numbers.

2024 carries the vibrational energy of the 8, which is a strong energy. It is a powerful, passive, feminine, yang and magnetic energy. The 8 energy is the Law of Attraction. You create, you believe, and do. Put out the idea and do the work and the 8 will attract and manifest for you. The 8 is an energy of abundance, so don't plan small. Go big for 2024!

ANGIE MCCOY, Scorpio, is a Transpersonal Life Coach, Intuitive Mentor, author, and course creator who utilizes tarot, astrology, and numerology to help clients develop a more expansive and interconnected sense of self in order to access their fullest potential. Using her areas of expertise, Angie helps women discover their True Self by breaking the barriers of their conditioned self so they can live an unconditionally fulfilled life with passion and on purpose. She offers a free introduction course on your Life Path, Personal Year & Personal Month numbers and energies.

www.AngieMcCoy.com | IG @angiemccoy.clc

Copyright © 2023 Tam Veilleux. All rights reserved worldwide.

From Our Contributors

OUT OF THE SHADOW

Every degree of the Zodiac and every Gate in Human Design presents us with a spectrum of energies ranging from high to low. It is up to each of us to choose at what level we are going to act. For example, Taurus energy can be very good at building something—a garden, a relationship, or financial well-being. However, in its lowest expression, Taurus can be fearful of living in poverty, get stuck in rigid patterns, and build upon weak foundations. Life presents us with opportunities, and we choose how we are going to show up.

Each week of the Energy Almanac, you are presented with possible shadow energies. The purpose is not for you to be in fear or judgment of yourself or others, but rather to gain perspective on the choices you get to make. How you respond to life's challenges and opportunities is where your free will lies. Becoming aware of the possible pitfalls helps you choose more carefully.

In part, the shadow energies come from my experience with The Gene Keys by Richard Rudd. The Gene Keys presents energy as a hologram where we can choose to be at the shadow, gift, or siddhi level—siddhi is a Sanskrit word meaning "the highest level." Much of the time, we unconsciously live in the shadow field where our fears drive our behavior. I hope that by bringing the potential shadows up to conscious awareness, we can become more deliberate in reaching higher vibrational frequencies.

How do we work with shadow energy? The first step is to read through the potential expression of the shadow energy for the week. Then step back and become the observer in your life. Is this shadow energy one you are familiar with? Do you struggle to release yourself from fear? Are there people or situations in your life that trigger a fear response? By stepping back, you can observe the answers to these questions from a neutral point of view. The next step is to prepare your response to these triggers should they arise. For example, if you face the fear of inadequacy, create a mini-dialogue to empower yourself. The opposite of inadequacy is wisdom. You could say to yourself, "I hold a depth of wisdom I can use in this situation."

Remember, you are in the driver's seat, and get to choose how you will move through fear and shadow energy!

JANET HICKOX, Gemini, is a gifted teacher, intuitive astrologer, and visionary who uses Astrology, Human Design, and the Gene Keys to help people live their authentic lives. Through a Human Design Astrology consult, she helps you unlock the key ingredients that make you unique, opening doors to freedom and success! A session with Janet gives you the valuable insight you need to make brilliant decisions in all areas of your life, including relationships, health, finances, and career. Janet believes, "To know oneself is priceless and leads to being in the right place, at the right time, with the right opportunities to thrive!"

www.living-astrology.com | IG @livingastrologywithjanet | FB @LivingAstrology

♡ Love the Energy Almanac? Tag us on social media: @TheEnergyAlmanac ♡
Copyright © 2023 Tam Veilleux. All rights reserved worldwide.

AROMATHERAPY & GEMSTONES

There is a certain alchemy that comes together when you combine the energetics of aromas and gemstones with astrology. Each of these elements on its own has the power to move you. Together, though, they create an undeniably potent aromatic and energetic elixir!

Each month in the Energy Almanac we are doing exactly that; we are presenting you with an aroma and a gemstone for the month along with suggestions on how to access their energies. So, as you set out to take aligned and intentional actions this year, you can choose to use each of these energetically alive elements on its own or you can combine them to curate your own unique daily ritual practice.

While you explore and discover the combinations of aromas and gemstones for each month, I want to remind you that everything is energy. We move through all kinds of energy every single day: positive, negative, and neutral. Aromatherapy and gemstones are simply (and magically) tools in your toolbox. They are tools that help you work in tandem with all of the energies that enter into our lives. Tools to inspire intentionality. Tools to help choose positivity. Additionally, while you work with the energies of the gemstones and aromas, remember that there is no wrong way to do this. Play! Tune into your intuition and get creative with your combinations!

Bring the aromas into your world by way of essential oils or stovetop potpourri. Beyond this, I encourage you to forage in the forest and to adorn your space with fresh cut flowers and fruits!

For the gemstones, speak to the energies and let the energies speak to you! Carry the stone in your pocket, wear it as jewelry, place it under your pillow or as the centerpiece of your space. The options are endless and you will know exactly what to do!

To go deeper, you are invited to join the Candle Club! When you join, each month I will send you an Intention Candle which is designed to pair with the month-by-month astrology forecasts, aromas, and gemstones found here in your Energy Almanac.

SARA HUGO, Scorpio, creates intention candles that are powered by her purpose to Make Magic Happen. She is deeply passionate about aligning action with intention and glitter is her favorite color! Those who know her often describe her superpowers as being able to tell you exactly what you need to hear exactly when you need to hear it and, unsurprisingly, as being the most intentional person they know. When Sara is not crafting candles, you can find her Building Joy with her clients and team as an Interior Designer & Sales Leader.

www.poppymountainrituals.com | IG @poppymountainrituals

Copyright © 2023 Tam Veilleux. All rights reserved worldwide.

TAROT FOR THE ZODIACS

Tarot cards have been used for centuries as a tool for spiritual guidance and self-discovery. Each card in the tarot deck represents a different archetype or energy and can be used to gain insight into our subconscious, our relationships, and our life path. The Tarot has been associated with astrology since its inception, with each card being connected to a particular planet, element, and zodiac sign.
Here are the tarot cards I have come to associate with each zodiac sign:

- Aries: The Emperor
- Taurus: The Hierophant
- Gemini: The Lovers
- Cancer: The Chariot
- Leo: Strength
- Virgo: The Hermit
- Libra: Justice
- Scorpio: Death
- Sagittarius: Temperance
- Capricorn: The Devil
- Aquarius: The Star
- Pisces: The Moon

As with astrology, these associations are not set in stone and may differ between readers and their personal reading styles as well as between different decks and the creator's artistic flair. These associations I provide here are intended to be a starting point for understanding the energies and archetypes that are aligned with each zodiac sign.

Each month you will find one Tarot card briefly described for the associated zodiac season along with the energetic impact that season may bring based on the card's archetypal meaning. Utilizing this information and working with each card for each season, you are able to be an active participant with the energetics and archetypes that guide us, and take inspired action towards the life you want. You may also gain deeper insight, awareness, and validation to who you are and wish to become.

I have also included an affirmation for each Tarot card as an added tool for your co-creation.

JEN SEROVY, Gemini, is a 1/3 Manifesting Generator, Gemini Sun, Pisces Moon, and a self-proclaimed Seeker, Mystic, Mentor. As a curious and continuous student of many spiritual modalities, she combines the skills and lessons learned in order to provide unique and custom guidance. It is with her deepest desire to help people cultivate a soul-led life that she holds space, witnesses, and supports the expansion of others as they show up authentically, aligned and fulfilled.

www.jenserovy.com | IG @jen.serovy | FB @jen.serovy

Copyright © 2023 Tam Veilleux. All rights reserved worldwide.

RITUALS & SPELLS

Merry Meet! You are full of sunbeams, starlight, mystery and, especially, magic. All of the mysteries of magic are within us all. Have you noticed? Have you felt your magical moments? Perhaps, you had a feeling, a thought and it found its way to reality. Did you wish upon a candle and blow it out with a deep breath? Did you recite a chant at the first star you saw in the night sky?

A simple magical ritual is a movement; a way to bring intentions to you through practiced movements. Knowledge of magic is within us all. All we need to do is coax it forward with intention. Magical elements are not supernatural, for is anything truly outside nature? Not only are we magical, magic is all around us.

Gather the natural elements held in all things and infuse your intentions to steer the magic. Simple guided rituals, spell jars and seasonal practices move your magic to support your intentions. Create your spell jars and rituals around seasonal celebrations. When you create a spell jar, you are sending out your magical intentions and desires. When you feel empowered or unsettled, when you know you need a magical boost, when you feel longing you cannot label. Design your daily rounds to be infused with magical practices and rituals.

While you move your magic, remember to harm none, seek good, and keep your magic personal. Do remember to not send out magic to those without their knowledge and consent. Use your magic well. Let your magic linger around you. Let your magic find you. Let your magic fill you. Merry Part!

LADY KARA, Cancer, is a Moon Child and practicing Hedge Witch. She collects the wisdom of herbs and plants to bring magic to the everyday using rituals and spells. Lady Kara draws simple magic in through guided rituals using nature, the elements and the seasons. Her magical specialities are spell jars and rituals. She knows that real magic is personal and not prescribed, therefore, she only offers gentle guidance and encouragement so each Newcomer may find their own path. As a Hedge Witch, she finds her magic in the simple everyday rounds in the home, kitchen, garden, and in nature. She is always willing to share her wisdom and magic.

nowforus7037@gmail.com

BONUS TOOLS & RESOURCES TO SUPPORT YOUR JOURNEY

WWW.CHOOSEBIGCHANGE.COM/PAGES/BONUS24

Copyright © 2023 Tam Veilleux. All rights reserved worldwide.

SELF-CARE

Self-care is a matter of great importance yet it never seems to be a top priority! There can be a million different reasons your self-care gets left out of your day, from not having enough time to being raised that you should put others first. Most of these reasons are just excuses but others lie deep in the subconscious and can be related to unhealed trauma and limiting beliefs. We often hear the phrase that "you can't pour from an empty cup" yet we feel guilty for prioritizing our own needs over others. I encourage taking such good care of yourself that others get what overflows out of your cup rather than draining your own goodness.

Self-care can often be misconstrued as a luxurious spa day but in reality, it is simply tuning into your intuition daily and seeing what you need to do in order to feel your best. At times in life, feeling your best can feel like a stretch, and on those days, I recommend asking yourself what you could do to bring a smile across your face or experience a moment of joy, satisfaction, or peace.

Self-care changes throughout the seasons and throughout your life. Your body, mind, and spirit will evolve as you age and need different things as time goes on. The information being shared with you monthly comes from the lens of Ayurveda and yogic philosophy. Ayurveda translates to the science of life. It factors in the dominant elements that are at play in your body and the environment according to the seasons. It is such a simple way to keep your body and mind in better balance throughout the year. I hope 2024 is a transformative and healing year full of self-care.

HILERY HUTCHINSON is a Scorpio 6/2 pure generator that follows her sacral authority to live the most joyful life possible. Hilery is on a mission to help people heal. She loves to help her clients improve their wellness in every aspect of life using the teachings of Ayurveda and Human Design. She brings a plethora of knowledge to her spiritual life coaching clients with over 55 certifications and 20 years of experience in the wellness industry. She has traveled around the world teaching in 14 different countries and now owns a retreat center in El Salvador.

www.healingwithhilery.com | IG @healingwithhilery
FB @healingwithhilery | fb.com/groups/healingwithhilery

Copyright © 2023 Tam Veilleux. All rights reserved worldwide.

FINANCES

HEALING YOUR SUBCONSCIOUS PARTS SO YOUR MONEY FLOWS

I'm big on learning the inner workings of the mind and you will hear me refer to Parts within the psyche. Think of Parts as the younger versions of you who need something. For instance, say at 3 years old you were abandoned or abused. At that point in time, developmentally, the young child cannot deal with that type of trauma, so it meticulously files that incident away in the deep recesses of its mind and body memory. This of course is a very good coping mechanism and keeps the 3-year-old alive. What happens later in life though, is that those memories, especially physical trauma memories, are still there, in the body and mind, taking over the adult's actions whenever it gets triggered. Think about a grown person who has anger issues. What age group typically has those types of meltdowns? Yes, you guessed it, 2 to 3-year-olds. The adult who has temper tantrums is typically acting out those 3-year-old stuck emotions. Heal that Part and the adult will flow through life much easier.

There are hundreds of Parts within and they all want a voice. On this month-by-month journey we will address some of those Parts so that you can get closer to the life you want to live, one that is full of money, freedom, love, and connection!

RHONDA HUNT MCCARTHY, Pisces, is a powerful spiritual healer, helping women of all ages embrace, heal, and learn from the parts of themselves that keep them in pain and repeating old patterns. She also offers help to clients who need to build a solid financial house so they can enjoy their retirement years. Outside of work, you will find Rhonda hanging out with those she loves, Mother Earth, and the big blue sea. She believes in love, freedom, and self-empowerment. Book a free strategy session with Rhonda today.

www.rhondahuntmccarthy.com | www.primerica.com/rhuntmccarthy

GET YOUR FREE BONUS CONTENT AT:
WWW.CHOOSEBIGCHANGE.COM/PAGES/BONUS24

Copyright © 2023 Tam Veilleux. All rights reserved worldwide.

LAUGHTER

Everyone wants health and happiness in their lives. But instead we are getting stressed out, depressed, getting less sleep, having more negative thoughts, and feeling isolated. Does this sound like you?

Did you know there is a way to change your mood within minutes by releasing certain chemicals from your brain called endorphins? There is a way to bring more oxygen into your body and brain, making you feel more energized and relaxed. Not only that, but by one simple practice, you will reduce your stress and strengthen your immune system, meaning you may not get sick easily and can possibly heal faster.

The answer? Laughter—yes, that thing we have been doing since around our fourth month of life. It is something we have within us at all times, it doesn't cost anything, and it is available 24/7. The reason is that during laughter, exhalation lasts much longer than in regular breathing. In normal breathing we inhale and exhale only 500 ml of air while there is 1500 ml of residual and stale air which has more than carbon dioxide. This can be forced by laughter exercises which bring more oxygen to our brain and body.

As you know, breath is life. One can live without food and water for several days, but cannot survive if breathing stops even for a few minutes. According to yogic philosophy, we are alive because the cosmic energy from the universe flows into the body through the breath, which is the life force or prana. Pranayama is the practice of breath regulation, and is a main component of yoga. In Sanskrit, *prana* means life energy and *yama* means control.

By creating a laughter practice, aka Laughter Yoga, you can refresh your body and spirit. Simple and profound, this practice is sweeping the world as a physical and mental refresher through a new type of exercise that stresses both without overtaxing either. Yoga gear not required!

Medical Disclaimer: Laughter Yoga is not a substitute for medical consultation for physical, mental and psychological illnesses, but it is a powerful natural complementary form of healing. It is like any other aerobic exercise and may not be suitable for everyone as it involves some physical strain and a rise in intra-abdominal pressure. Should you experience any discomfort, please discontinue and get medical advice.

LARISSA JOHNSON, Capricorn. Larissa or *la risa* means laughter in Spanish and French. It is thought to be derived from the Latin *hilaris*, which means cheerful. And with a name like that, how can you not radiate positivity and happiness? As a self-proclaimed EDUTAINER, she has made it her mission to illuminate serious topics in a fun and entertaining way.

larissajohnson.com | IG @laughinglarissa

Copyright © 2023 Tam Veilleux. All rights reserved worldwide.

READER BONUSES

FREE GIFTS FOR YOU

Each year collaborators for the Energy Almanac come together to share their personal brilliance. Each amazing contributor brings their own special variety of wisdom. We at Choose Big Change want you to go deeper, reach further, be intimately entwined with their work. Go to this link in your web browser:

HTTPS://CHOOSEBIGCHANGE.COM/PAGES/BONUS24

Here you will find a large selection of bonus offers for you to apply to your life. Some are free, many are discounts, all are delightful!

Scroll through the robust list of available offerings from our collaborators and take all those that resonate with you. These are their gifts to you for 2024.

Copyright © 2023 Tam Veilleux. All rights reserved worldwide.

UNDERSTAND YOUR TRUE SELF & LIVE YOUR BEST LIFE!

Get Your Personalized FREE Human Design Astrology Chart and Report

Learn:

- how to make the best decisions for you
- how to have successful relationships
- how to use your energy in a healthy and sustainable way

GO TO: WWW.LIVING-ASTROLOGY.COM

2024 GIFT GIVING

FAMILY FLOCK ZODIAC ART

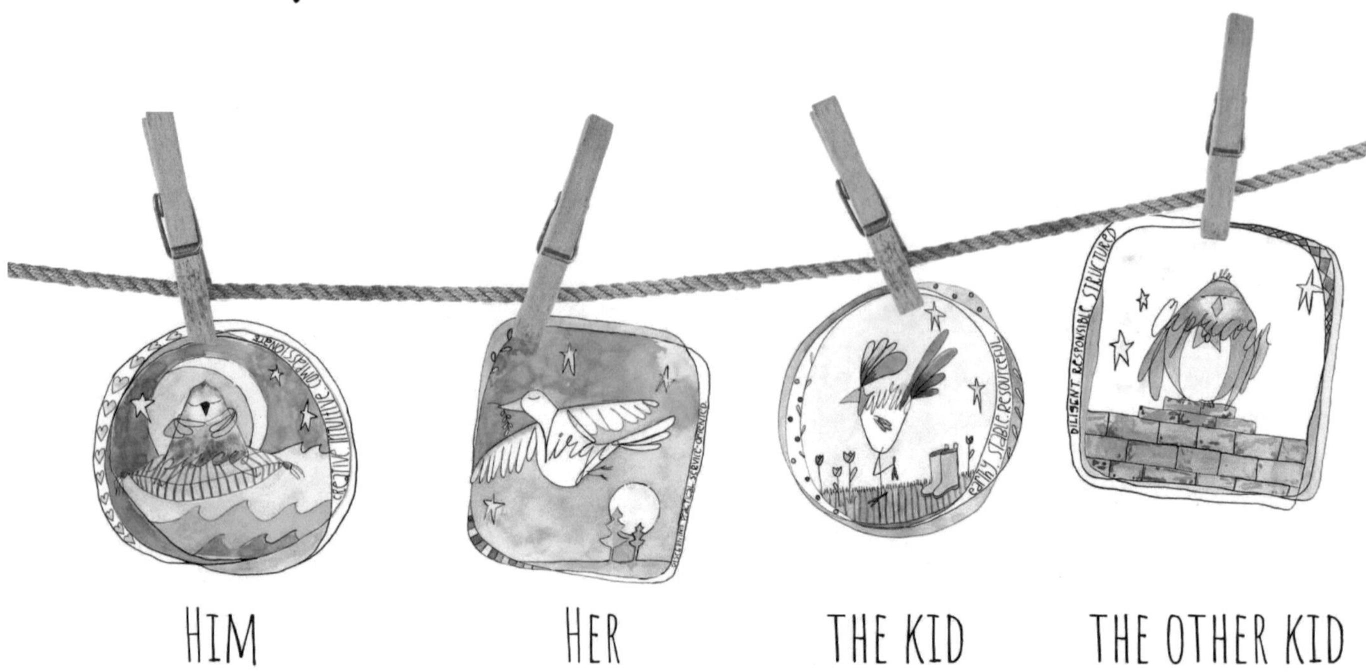

Do you love the illustrations in this year's Energy Almanac?

Get your zodiac bird + words illustration as downloadable 4" x 4" prints for framing or pinning. These colorful conversation starters make a great presentation.

BUY. PRINT. CLIP. FRAME.

HTTPS://CHOOSEBIGCHANGE.COM/COLLECTIONS/GIFT-GIVING

January

COMMITMENT TOWARD SPIRITUALITY

JANUARY 1-7

DO choose your battles wisely.
DO NOT focus on fear of survival.

JANUARY 8-14

DO bring order to new information that arrives.
DO NOT stay locked in old fear-based patterns.

JANUARY 15-21

DO focus attention on your heart space.
DO NOT stay stuck in anxious thoughts.

JANUARY 22-28

DO look ahead to what you want to do this year.
DO NOT jump at opportunities yet.

IT'S SAFE FOR ME TO EXPECT GREAT EXPERIENCES THIS YEAR.

JANUARY 11, 6:57 AM EST

NEW MOON AT 20° CAPRICORN
TAKING MEANINGFUL ACTION

JANUARY 25, 12:54 PM EST

FULL MOON AT 5° LEO
SERIOUS ABOUT PLAY

Copyright © 2023 Tam Veilleux. All rights reserved worldwide.

January

Ahh, a new year begins and we collectively have reason to feel hopeful about the twelve months ahead. It's a clean slate once again. Mercury is going to come out of its retrograde in the optimistic sign of Sagittarius and we can communicate our expanded vision for the future. Perfect timing for January, wouldn't you say? With an abundance of incoming light from sextile luminaries Jupiter in Taurus and Saturn in Pisces you'll notice opportunities for spiritual healing and high expectations. You've surely tightened up your spiritual practices in 2023 and in 2024 you will carry those forward by diligently applying them to the goals you set this month. Be mindful of Mars energy—it can be aggressive or passionate, but only you can determine that outflow. The Capricorn New Moon is perfectly situated to set you up for the business of life. You can feel free to think big and create a plan that you can then apply to the rest of the year while always remembering to course correct as needed.

When Pluto, the planet of regeneration, slips into the forward-thinking sign of Aquarius for a lengthy two-decade stay, you can expect your subconscious mind to play with ideas concerning innovation, freedom, and humanitarianism. There's a long period of change coming around those topics and you will surely play your part over these next twenty years. For this month, it's "eyes wide open" to possibilities that will surely present themselves. Don't be afraid of change, Little Pretzel, it's the only thing you can surely count on.

BOOK BONUSES INCLUDE DISCOUNT CODES, EBOOKS, SPECIAL REPORTS, AUDIO FILES AND SPECIAL OFFERS. TO GET ALL THE GOODIES, GO TO
WWW.CHOOSEBIGCHANGE.COM/PAGES/BONUS24

KEY DATES

1/1 **Mercury stations direct in Sagittarius**
1/14 **Mars enters Capricorn**
1/11 **New Moon in Capricorn,** read moon article
1/13 **Mercury enters Capricorn**
1/20 **Happy Birthday, Aquarians**
1/22 **Pluto enters Aquarius**
1/23 **Venus enters Capricorn**
1/24 **Jupiter sextile Saturn** until February 17
1/25 **Full Moon in Leo,** read moon article
1/26 **Uranus stations direct in Taurus**

♡ Fun, fresh, transformational products + services: https://choosebigchange.com ♡

Copyright © 2023 Tam Veilleux. All rights reserved worldwide.

JANUARY PREDICTIONS

MONDAY, JANUARY 1 – SUNDAY, JANUARY 7

MOONS: VIRGO, LIBRA, SCORPIO

Happy new year to you! As we enter the first day of the first week of the year, Mercury will station direct in the sign of Sagittarius. Don't expect instant gratification. The depositor of communication needs several more days before information concerning your truths can be clearly communicated. Also on day one, Venus in Sagittarius wrestles with Saturn in Pisces. Your urge for adventure and movement could be squelched by the feeling of obedience and duty to your spiritual practices. Compromise with yourself; it could be a day to both pray and play. Toward the end of the week on Thursday Mars, planet of action, will move into Capricorn. Here begins a period of slower, more thoughtful actions—think: harnessed energy for getting things done. The moons of the week are Virgo, Libra, Scorpio.

GIFT & SHADOW THIS WEEK: *Choose your battles wisely this week. That means if something is worth fighting for, it is appropriate to continue, and if it is not worth it, then time to free yourself from the struggle. We are also closing out a phase in our collective destiny which requires that we redefine the meaning of success. Is success really about how much money you make or how far up the ladder you go? Can you find a deeper connection to success?*

MONDAY, JANUARY 8 – SUNDAY, JANUARY 14

MOONS: SAGITTARIUS, CAPRICORN, AQUARIUS, PISCES

This week opens with Mercury in Sagittarius squaring up to Neptune in Pisces. Being a straight-shooter with your words these days means that you could find yourself needing to bite your tongue for a few days when it comes to sharing your thoughts around faith. Leave room for other opinions, right? Tuesday's multi-planet transits involve the Sun trine Uranus and a Mars-Saturn sextile. This urges you to plan and bring order to sudden new insights or information that arrives, especially where it concerns large groups, humanitarian efforts, or technology. The midweek moon in Capricorn is all business. Be sure to read our moon article, seek solitude, and enjoy the light. As the second week of the year winds down Mars trines Jupiter, still in Taurus for half of this year. Now you can spend time progressing plans for your resources. Maybe you'll look out at the rest of 2024 and see how and when you might invest, leverage, or save money. It's also a good time to take responsibility for your own self-worth.

GIFT & SHADOW THIS WEEK: *The shadow energy this week revolves around survival, specifically our fear that we won't survive. Blessedly there is a simple way around this energy and that is to focus on the light. We are entering a time of releasing the more tribal fears we have and that is by creating an initiation into a new way of being together on the planet. Difficult? Not so much unless we stubbornly stay locked in old patterns of fear instead of letting ourselves be free of them.*

Copyright © 2023 Tam Veilleux. All rights reserved worldwide.

MONDAY, JANUARY 15 – SUNDAY, JANUARY 21	**MOONS:** PISCES, ARIES, TAURUS, GEMINI

Week three starts with your imagination and faith lighting the way. You may find yourself lost in thoughts about your goals for 2024. Tuesday and Wednesday your mind may be busy organizing ideas about technology or humanitarian progress. Take notes, and expand on those ruminations on Friday when Jupiter joins the party to bring a feeling of hope to your concepts' outcomes. It's surely a day of conflict though, because also present are Venus in Sagittarius square Neptune in Pisces. Venus wants to speak her truth and it may not come out sounding sweet. Truth well-spoken can be beneficial, but the chance of whining about your victimhood, or staying stuck in your old philosophies about religion or faith is also present. Friday is a good day to practice your listening skills and focus on those ideas from earlier in the week. Let the weekend run its course with your mind firmly seeking answers concerning where change can happen.

GIFT & SHADOW THIS WEEK: *If you find yourself in fear and worry this week, then you have succumbed to the shadow energy of the week. Likely you have been too much in your head instead of being in the heart, and that is where anxiety can niggle away at your sanctity. In the highest of this energy, we are attuned to what is needed and we trust everything is exactly as it needs to be. Mind the details, but don't let them overwhelm you.*

MONDAY, JANUARY 22 – SUNDAY, JANUARY 28	**MOONS:** GEMINI, CANCER, LEO, VIRGO

January 22nd is a big day in astrology as Pluto, the bringer of powerful regeneration, enters the sign of Aquarius. You're beginning a twenty-year stretch heralding the changing landscape of technology, innovation, and how we handle each other. Groups. Tribes. Families. No longer will society tolerate "It's good for me." For the next two decades it'll be "It's good for WE." These changes trickle into society in earnest in 2024 as Pluto enters the first degree.

Mid-week Venus, planet of love and money, puts on the three-piece suit of Capricorn and if ever you thought a business partner might benefit you, this could be a time when that idea comes to fruition. You'll enjoy the disciplined approach to budgeting and relationship through the first week of March. But for now, focus on the Full Moon in Leo on Thursday. High drama? Maybe. Read the moon article!

Starting on January 26th, Jupiter sextiles Saturn and you are in for a long run of opportunity and happy outlooks. Jupiter is wearing the denim overalls of Taurus, expanding your resources as well as your values and self-worth. Now we find him skipping across the cosmos with his old buddy Saturn, the Cosmic Thumb. Pressure is applied toward using resources toward good causes and new, unique ideas. This is a time period worth watching! Opportunities will present themselves and you have the authority and autonomy to make right decisions that can create abundance for yourself (and maybe others). The sextile between Jupiter and Saturn will end February 17th. Stay alert to possibilities and the right timing for saying yes.

Friday through Sunday bring some busy planets. A leader with a unique perspective has concerns about wealth and the accumulation of holdings. There could be a confrontation, but there certainly will be tension around the topic. Hopefully you keep an open mind and allow Uranus to bring sudden insights that can create a shift in

♡ Fun, fresh, transformational products + services: https://choosebigchange.com ♡

Copyright © 2023 Tam Veilleux. All rights reserved worldwide.

thinking or a rewriting of the plan you've held dear. Sunday is the day for planning, planning, planning as long as you're keeping your eyes open for blind spots. Remember to always be willing to course correct.

GIFT & SHADOW THIS WEEK: *Happy Human Design New Year (on January 22nd)! While we celebrate a new year in the Human Design System, it is still a time for connecting to the dreamtime. Dreamtime is the pause between being and doing. Take time to look ahead at what you want to do this year, but don't take steps yet. Consider where you might need to make some changes and how you might want to grow and evolve into the year. In the shadow this week, we may "jump" at opportunities and find ourselves having to reel back in from being overly impulsive.*

ENERGY ALMANAC CALL TO ACTION: Did you have an a-ha moment this month? If so, be brave! Employ your courage and share your insights on social media. Tag @TheEnergyAlmanac so we can cheer you on!

Heavily Meditated Journal

A GOOD NOTEBOOK CAN HELP YOU WITH MOTIVATION TO TAKE MORE NOTES, WRITE DOWN IDEAS, OR LIST FUTURE DREAMS. THIS CUSTOM, WIRE-BOUND NOTEBOOK WILL BE A GREAT DAILY COMPANION WHENEVER YOU NEED TO PUT YOUR THOUGHTS DOWN ON PAPER!

SEVERAL COVER DESIGNS TO CHOOSE FROM.

WWW.CHOOSEBIGCHANGE.COM

Copyright © 2023 Tam Veilleux. All rights reserved worldwide.

JANUARY 11, 6:57 AM EST
NEW MOON AT 20° CAPRICORN

TAKING MEANINGFUL ACTION

Is there a better time to get stuff done than a Capricorn new moon? For starters, the new moon inherently carries the energy of new beginnings. Capricorn loves to take action, see progress, and fulfill a purpose.

All our closest planets are in signs that demand momentum. Mercury and Venus are in Sagittarius, and Mars is in Capricorn, too. This is a lot of grounding, ambitious energy. Let's use it wisely by putting rubber on the road.

It doesn't matter what your first action is, just take it. Capricorn energy will carry you from there because it builds momentum effortlessly. Reverse engineer your future dreams to see what seeds you need to plant now.

Start with the end in mind to make the most of your efforts. What is the biggest dream you can dream? Write it down, along with everything else you'll need to do to get there. Busy Capricorn will be excited to tackle that to-do list.

AFFIRMATION: ***"I take meaningful action towards my dreams every day, even if it's small."***

MONTHLY MOONWORK:

- Create a mind map outlining all the action steps you will (eventually) take to manifest your dreams.
- Take your very first action! Then pat yourself on the back.
- Keep taking purposeful action, even if it's purposeful rest.

♡ Fun, fresh, transformational products + services: https://choosebigchange.com ♡

Copyright © 2023 Tam Veilleux. All rights reserved worldwide.

JANUARY 25, 12:54 PM EST

FULL MOON AT 5° LEO

SERIOUS ABOUT PLAY

Leo is loud and proud, always eager to experience as much of life as possible. The energy right now is bright, just like Luna herself. However, there's a stern side to the playfulness. As Saturn in Pisces is in a testy relationship with the Moon, we're being guided to take a serious look at how much fun we are having. Saturn wants us to recognize the importance of fun for relaxation. And to make room for it.

Use this energy to let go of whatever isn't bringing you fun and joy (finally!). Just because we're (mostly) grown up doesn't mean we can't have fun. What good is all the hard work we do if we aren't enjoying ourselves?

How do you love to play? There's gaming, pretending, creating, running, dancing, exploring, or anything else that suits you. Replace what's not working with playtime, because it's not working anyway! Nothing fills your cup more than doing what brings you joy.

AFFIRMATION: ***"I prioritize and embrace playtime! It's easy to find time to do what I love."***

MONTHLY MOONWORK:

- Think back to your favorite childhood games or hobbies, and go discover if you still love them.
- What are your daily priorities? What can you afford to stop doing so you can play instead?
- Challenge yourself to experience a brand new way to have fun with something you've never done before.

☆ Get your book bonus offers: www.choosebigchange.com/pages/bonus24 ☆

Copyright © 2023 Tam Veilleux. All rights reserved worldwide.

Numerology

January starts the year out with its 1, representing the first month, blended with the 8 year giving us a 9 energy (1 + 8 = 9). It's almost an oxymoron—the new year and new beginnings starts with endings and completion of the 9. At the same time, it aligns with our traditions of "Out with the old, in with the new" for ringing in the new year. The endings and completion energy of the 9 is all about letting go of things that no longer serve us and/or transformation of those things. It's a great vibe to begin the new year, if you work with the energy. Take some time this month to evaluate your life and see what needs to be released and what changes you can make to create transformation to ignite that attraction energy of the 8 of abundance in 2024.

Aromatherapy & Gemstones

AROMAS: SAGE & CYPRESS The new year opens by asking us to begin again and to greet it with a renewed sense of optimism. It is the perfect time to enhance your positivity by incorporating the grounding and cleansing fragrances of Sage & Cypress into your daily routines.

Sage is a calming green leaf often used for its soothing properties during ancient practice of burning dried plants to remove negative or stagnant energy. Sage, paired with the earthy and grounding fragrance of cypress, will cleanse your space and your aura; it will allow you to release the past, ground into the present, and embrace all that is yet to come.

Immerse yourself in these centering properties and set yourself up to be in a space to begin again and create the life you desire.

GEMSTONE: MOONSTONE As January welcomes us into the arms of its new year, we become aware of and in tune with, the cyclical nature of life. In this time of new beginnings, we are reminded that change is the only constant.

This month, it is important to embrace the flow of the bigger energies of change that are in play rather than sinking into overwhelm. Moonstone crystals are powerful stones that embody feminine and divine wisdom. This stone encourages balance, healing, and comfort in times of change.

Moonstone will support you by tapping into the flow to help you manage change effectively and to appropriately express your emotions. Enjoy the pleasures of life. Create freely. Be sensitive, intuitive, and abstract. Open up and allow the possibility for nature's purpose to flow through you. Like the moon in the sky, the power of Moonstone crystals is in its divine energy; let it light your way forward.

ACCESS THE ENERGIES:

- Place a few drops of Cypress essential oil in your hands. Cup your palms at your face and nose. Breathe deeply.
- Perform a smudge ritual using Sage & Cypress to cleanse your space and aura.
- Keep a Moonstone crystal in your pocket or wear a piece of jewelry to bring you comfort in times of change throughout the day.

♡ Fun, fresh, transformational products + services: https://choosebigchange.com ♡

Copyright © 2023 Tam Veilleux. All rights reserved worldwide.

The tarot card associated with Capricorn is **The Devil**. This card is often misunderstood, and is not necessarily a negative card. It represents the darker side of human nature and the challenges that we must face in order to overcome our fears and limitations. It can symbolize temptation and addiction, but also determination to break free from these negative patterns and take control of our lives.

In Capricorn season, you may be prone to being overly critical or hard on yourself, and this card can remind you to let go of those self-imposed limitations and embrace your true and highest potential. This is also a reminder to stay grounded and focused on our goals, even when faced with obstacles and temptations.

THE DEVIL AFFIRMATION ***"I face my shadow with confidence and grace, and allow myself to navigate challenges confidently and reach my goals without limitations."***

MINDFUL TEA RITUAL

Merry Meet! The New Year, a season of beginnings, hopes, new dreams. A promise of change you made for yourself. Your mind races, filled with the plans of actions to take, next steps, outlines, schedules. The bustle of change takes hold, you charge forward. It takes just a blink and you are overwhelmed, the need to reset and clarify your purpose settles in. You know you must get still and find your center. You prepare a Mindful Tea Ritual.

RITUAL: Select the cup that calls to you. Today, it may be a delicate bone china cup with saucer, perhaps a handmade earthenware vessel with Celtic symbols, a mug that feels like it belongs in your hands. You will know which cup when your eyes smile after it is chosen. You may feel called to use your favorite teapot, the one with all the memories and feelings. If so, bring it out. Choose your tea. Set a kettle to boil. When the kettle sings, you are ready. Pour boiling water into your cup and pot. Hold the vessel close with both hands. Feel the warmth as it spreads through to your hands. Breathe in goodness, breathe out to release. Empty the water from your vessel.

Set your intentions as you add tea and boiling water to your vessel. As you speak your intentions, stir slowly. Stir three times clockwise to bring positive intentions, stir three times counterclockwise to banish negative influences.

Stir your intentions should you add sweetener or cream.

- Settle into a sacred, peaceful space. A space where you feel light, that feels promising.
- Hold your vessel with both hands, softly close your eyes, breathe in, breathe out, 3 times, as you bring your intentions into focus. Open your eyes and with each sip, say your intentions.
- When your tea is done, rinse your cup, swirling the water 3 times, following your intentions.

Come back to your Mindful Tea Ritual as often as you are called to.

Merry Part!

✯ Get your book bonus offers: www.choosebigchange.com/pages/bonus24 ✯

Copyright © 2023 Tam Veilleux. All rights reserved worldwide.

Self-care

It's a brand new year so let's get off to a fresh start by learning how to shower. Did you know you may be doing it all wrong?! According to Ayurvedic philosophy, there are two steps to take before you even get into the shower. First, you dry brush to get all the dead skin off of your body before it gets wet. This will also increase your energy levels and boost your immune system. Then you use oil to perform an abyangha massage to protect your skin from the hot water. To learn how, go to the bonus page and follow the self-care link.

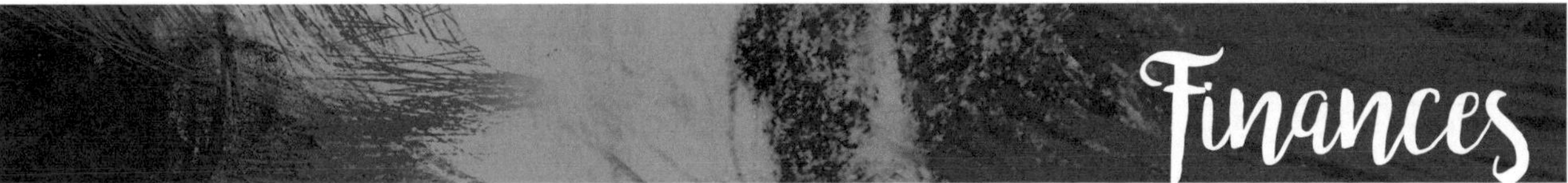

Finances

Money can be an elusive energy and at the same time, it can bring the freedom to put your innovative ideas to work for the greater good and fulfill that humanitarian side of yours. In order to open up to your possibilities it would be good for you to get to know your Parts. Some hold certain money ideas they learned as you grew and since January is a clean slate, I encourage you, with your eyes wide open, to do an exercise that will get you closer to your Parts and discover what their driving thoughts are on the money subject. Remember, as you think big, don't be afraid of change and course correct as you need to.

Take out your You're The One Journal and begin to capture the words you think and say about money. This can be tricky because you don't always think about what you're thinking and saying, it is very automatic. Become aware, capture, and see the patterns that are so latently imbued into your mind's system.

Go to the Energy Almanac Bonus Page (www.choosebigchange.com/pages/bonus24) to get your free, You're The One Journal, which includes a wheel of life assessment with explanation.

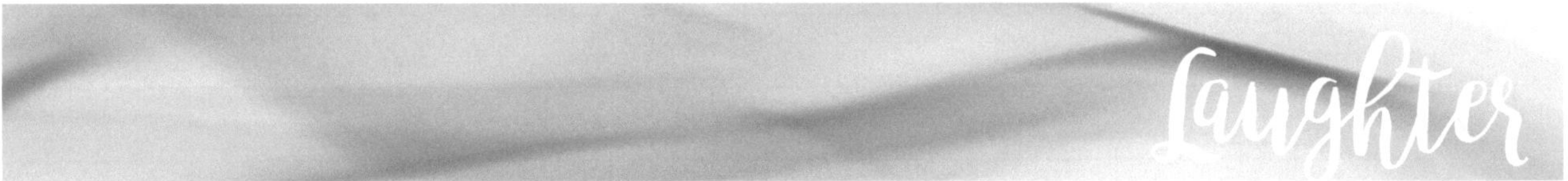

Laughter

It's a new year, the time for resolutions. What if you just resolve to laugh more? It wouldn't take that much time out of your day and it will start to make you feel better to tackle those other resolutions you want to complete.

This month, we will be doing the **#40DayLaughterChallenge**—yes you read that correctly! We will be laughing for one minute every day for 40 days!

No sense of humor? No worries, fake it! According to a 2010 report in *Alternative Therapies in Health and Medicine* by Ramon Mora-Ripoli, the human brain is unable to distinguish spontaneous laughter from self-induced so pretending to laugh can produce the same health-related benefits as the real thing.

For the next 40 days, I want you to laugh for one minute straight for absolutely no reason. It can be real laughter; it can be fake laughter. It can be videotaped and shared on your social media channels (if so, please tag me on Instagram @LaughingLarissa) or it can be done just for yourself. All you have to do is set a timer and go!

Copyright © 2023 Tam Veilleux. All rights reserved worldwide.

✯ Get your book bonus offers: www.choosebigchange.com/pages/bonus24 ✯

Copyright © 2023 Tam Veilleux. All rights reserved worldwide.

February

OPPORTUNITIES AND ACTION

JANUARY 29 – FEBRUARY 4

DO practice self-love.
DO NOT cling to codependency.

FEBRUARY 5 – 11

DO notice where you've overcome adversity.
DO NOT dismiss the power of gratitude.

FEBRUARY 12 – 18

DO be thoughtful in what you say yes to.
DO NOT over commit.

FEBRUARY 19 – 25

DO break free from victim thinking.
DO NOT be blind to timing issues.

FEBRUARY 26 – MARCH 3

DO not be impetuous.
DO NOT make agreements which are out of integrity.

IT IS SAFE FOR ME TO EXPAND MY VISION AND TAKE WELL-CALCULATED RISKS.

FEBRUARY 9, 5:59 PM EST

SUPER NEW MOON AT 20° AQUARIUS
CULTIVATE SOCIAL CHANGE

FEBRUARY 24, 7:30 AM EST

FULL MOON AT 5° VIRGO
CHOOSE NON-JUDGMENT

Copyright © 2023 Tam Veilleux. All rights reserved worldwide.

February

Lucky you! As February opens, the potential opportunities due to Jupiter and Saturn's hand-holding means there's still a chance for doors to open in your favor. There is more room for risk taking and expanded prosperity. You can keep the rose-colored glasses on for a bit longer, or at least until the 19th of the month. Life is expanding and positive attitudes prevail, so enjoy the ride for a little longer.

Mid-month will bring the urge to act. When Mars squares Pluto you may feel ready to be bold and lead the rebellion. I hear you asking, "What rebellion?" Only you know that answer. Available to you from February 21-23 are Venus and Mars skipping together through the cosmos in the sign of Aquarius. A feeling of balanced action for the benefit of all will present itself. You may experience a smoother relationship, innovative ideas, and intuitive insights that will effectively fuel the future. Yay for planetary hand-holding!

In the final week of February, the luminaries are busy! A stellium (which is when there are multiple planets in close contact with one another) forms on February 28th in the sign of Pisces. This day is meant for your spiritual growth. You (Sun) should block time (Saturn) that day to think (Mercury) about your relationship to creativity, intuition, compassion, and spirituality. You should actively contemplate your vision for your life. Expand that vision the next day by writing about it in your journal. These two dates aren't without their own challenges. Mars, the aggressive athlete, goes toe-to-toe with Jupiter. You may feel the tension between wanting to move on something while feeling that resources shouldn't be abused. You may need to let things simmer for a bit while things sort themselves out; the vision is expanding, but timing is everything.

BOOK BONUSES INCLUDE DISCOUNT CODES, EBOOKS, SPECIAL REPORTS, AUDIO FILES AND SPECIAL OFFERS. TO GET ALL THE GOODIES, GO TO
WWW.CHOOSEBIGCHANGE.COM/PAGES/BONUS24

KEY DATES

2/1	**Jupiter sextile Saturn through February 17**
2/6	**Mercury enters Aquarius**
2/9	**New Moon in Aquarius,** read moon article
2/14	**Mars enters Aquarius**
2/16	**Venus enters Aquarius**
2/20	**Happy Birthday, Pisceans**
2/24	**Full Moon in Virgo,** read moon article
2/24	**Mercury enters Pisces**
2/28	**Stellium in Pisces**

♡ Fun, fresh, transformational products + services: https://choosebigchange.com ♡

Copyright © 2023 Tam Veilleux. All rights reserved worldwide.

FEBRUARY PREDICTIONS

MONDAY, JANUARY 29 – SUNDAY, FEBRUARY 4

MOONS: VIRGO, LIBRA, SCORPIO, SAGITTARIUS

With Pluto firmly in Aquarius, the transformation of humanitarian efforts is finally beginning. Hold onto your panties, Little Pretzel, this twenty-year transit is meant to do everyone good. Also present as we start February, is the continuation of Jupiter's sextile to Saturn where last month we recommended that you keep your eyes and ears open for opportunities to use your resources in new and innovative ways.

Mercury, planet of the lower mind, currently in the ever-serious sign of Capricorn, will tickle Neptune on Friday. Here, spiritual ideas can meld with business planning. Take a look at timing and responsibilities and new ways of employing your altar. Enjoy some optimism and a little adventure for the weekend.

GIFT & SHADOW THIS WEEK: *We all want to feel like we belong in a family, tribe, or community. The shadow this week concerns when that need turns into neediness, clinginess or codependency. Increasing our heart-to-heart connections with others begins from a healthy sense of self-worth, self-love, and value. We might also need to watch out for re-telling old stories of abandonment, "nobody wants me," or other negative narratives. You belong, you are worthy, and you are valued!*

MONDAY, FEBRUARY 5 – SUNDAY, FEBRUARY 11

MOONS: SAGITTARIUS, CAPRICORN, AQUARIUS, PISCES

This week on Monday, Mercury, in his final degree of Capricorn, conjuncts Pluto. Here you have the chance to consider the transformation of yourself as an individual in hopes of contributing well to the collective. What can you do, who can you be that will benefit the greater WE? Block time to do the contemplation well because on Tuesday, Mercury will enter the first degree of Aquarius where he will enjoy creative, fast-moving thoughts. Mid-week when the Sun squares Uranus, there's a contest. Will you, or some principal with unique ideas, plow forward or will resources be used in a traditional manner? Venus is flavoring the days with an energy of abundance, perhaps suggesting, "There's enough for all of us" while Mars and Neptune continue the discussion of adding disciplined action to your spirituality. With Saturday comes the potential tangle between acts of autonomy and self-worth issues. This inner conversation can be journaled thoughtfully for outcomes that help your self-growth.

GIFT & SHADOW THIS WEEK: *Have you gotten stuck in old patterns or are you finding it hard to transform yourself or something in your life? If so, then this week is for you! The highest gift in this week is really about gratitude and seeing the blessings in our lives, even when the blessings come because we have had to make a change. Sometimes we can even get stuck rationalizing why we need to settle for less—No way! Allow yourself to find your arc of success in all things. You deserve it! Redefine your stories to include how you traversed adversity to emerge into the light.*

ENERGY ALMANAC CALL TO ACTION: Post on your social media your ideas for transforming the world's ways of handling groups of people. Tag @TheEnergyAlmanac in your post.

Copyright © 2023 Tam Veilleux. All rights reserved worldwide.

MONDAY, FEBRUARY 12 – SUNDAY, FEBRUARY 18

MOONS: PISCES, ARIES, TAURUS, GEMINI

Spirituality and commitment are at the front of your thoughts as this week opens and your personal power to change and take ownership of those changes are also influencing your reflections. On Valentine's Day, impress your sweetheart with powerful acts of kindness. Perhaps buy a bouquet and rather than hand the entire thing over to your partner at the restaurant, hand out one blossom to each of the individuals near you? If that doesn't knock their socks off and make them melt, nothing will!

On Saturday, Venus enters Aquarius for a short tour. Notice a friendly disposition and an urge for unity while upholding the individual's uniqueness. The weekend may find you dwelling on how we all can best use our resources in new ways. Analyze various approaches to creating the needed transformation. There's a little edge of "I'd rather things stay the same," but with applied strong communication skills you may be able to start a movement. Be the change and lead the change you wish to see in this world.

GIFT & SHADOW THIS WEEK: *Do you find yourself saying "yes" to everything, and then when that one thing comes along that you really want to participate in, you find you're bogged down and don't have the time, energy, or resources to participate? This week's gift is saying "yes" to the right things rather than everything. And, what are the right things? The ones that you are passionate about or that align you with joy and vitality rather than heaviness and obligation.*

MONDAY, FEBRUARY 19 – SUNDAY, FEBRUARY 25

MOONS: CANCER, LEO, VIRGO

The third week of February is your final chance to glimpse possibilities offered by Jupiter and Saturn's sextile. Look back over the last few weeks now. What opportunities might you have glanced over? The transit is winding down, grab the low hanging fruit, will you?

Use Wednesday through Friday for expressing and acting upon your individual desires. Your ideas have merit. Your intuitive hits could be strong but don't be blind to timing. Act only when appropriate, it's best not to let your passion get ahead of you. On Saturday, Mercury, the communicator, will enter Pisces. Note the softer, kinder communication style and an amplified inner voice. Your intuition is alert and creative endeavors are afoot. It's a good way to wrap up the cold final weeks of winter in the United States. Pick an artistic hobby and work with it to stave off boredom. The weekend is also full of consternation about money, Venus wants to have a fair and intellectual conversation about what you value while Jupiter's pie-in-the-sky ideas seem off-base. Patience is needed. These are only ideas and points of view—there's no need to decide anything.

GIFT & SHADOW THIS WEEK: *The gift of abundance is ours not because of what we do but because of who we are—Divine Beings. The gift energy this week reminds us of this reality. Unfortunately, we have built an entire society around doing and getting paid for what we do. This minimizes the blessings of our intrinsic value. We then become more like "human doings" rather than human beings. This week, there is also fear and worry that we are not "enough" or will fail to be enough or have enough. Choose freedom from victim thinking.*

♡ Fun, fresh, transformational products + services: https://choosebigchange.com ♡

Copyright © 2023 Tam Veilleux. All rights reserved worldwide.

MONDAY, FEBRUARY 26 – SUNDAY, MARCH 3

MOONS: VIRGO, LIBRA, SCORPIO, SAGITTARIUS

As you close out February, the desire for passionate action may bump up against the economy or your personal resources. Should you spend the money? Is there a way to do the deed while managing your assets or is this about your self-worth? Are you not feeling confident about your resources? Either way, don't be impetuous.

This week holds an important astrological transit. The stellium in Pisces brings an abundance of energy meant to tip us all in the same direction—that being communicating and living from a place of spirituality and creativity. Mercury, Sun, and Saturn all beg for your attention to spiritual discipline, spiritual listening, and soulful behaviors. You create your own reality and this day seems deemed for dreaming into it. The rub is Mars square Jupiter on the same day. Mars wants you to act for the good of all and Jupiter is minding the billfold and the file of stories about deservedness. For the good of everyone, do the work of discovering why you don't feel up to par. What story is holding you back? Do yourself a favor and tell a new story. As the stellium directs us, we are creators of our own realities. The opportunity to relive an old, worn-out idea is upon you. When the last days of this month close, find yourself communicating soulfully and about your value system and the need for more discipline or self-authority. See—we told you to do the inner work! Feel hopeful. You can (and will) feel better about your position in the world. The Sun is rising on you now!

March 1-3 suggests a leader, maybe you, feels cheerful. The rose-colored glasses are on and hope fills the air before Saturday when you may need to seek answers about the changing landscape of your personal economy.

GIFT & SHADOW THIS WEEK: *Broken deals can lead to broken hearts this week. We are challenged to keep our agreements and contracts. Of course, agreements have to begin in integrity. The gift is when we keep our commitments and agreements, we have peace both personally and collectively. Make honest and aligned agreements with others, keep your word, be honest, and peace will be the result. There is also an element this week of a lack mentality when we don't keep our agreements. That is part of an old paradigm whose time has come to be eliminated.*

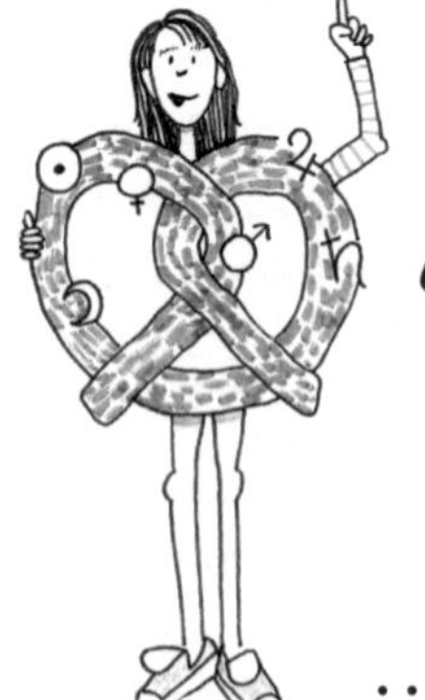

GET THE MATCHING ENERGY ALMANAC JOURNAL FOR CAPTURING ALL OF YOUR THOUGHTS. IT IS AVAILABLE AT OUR ONLINE STORE. PLEASE VISIT:

WWW.CHOOSEBIGCHANGE.COM/PRODUCTS/2024-JOURNAL

Copyright © 2023 Tam Veilleux. All rights reserved worldwide.

February Moons

FEBRUARY 9, 5:59 PM EST
SUPER NEW MOON AT 20° AQUARIUS

Aquarius is the rebel who breaks the rules for the good of the many. With the Sun, Moon, and Mercury all in Aquarius, now's our chance to brainstorm creative solutions to social issues. Maintain an open mind because you never know where groundbreaking inspiration will come from.

This new moon is starting a much larger cycle beyond just this lunation. It's the first of four super new moons in a row, one of which is a total solar eclipse. The build-up of energy will reach a crescendo in April. The seeds you plant now will take many moon cycles to manifest. Perfect for Aquarius who is determined to dismantle and rebuild society so it's more supportive of the collective.

Jupiter and Mercury are taking a moment to warn us about over-promising and under-delivering. We all dream of a better future for humanity but be realistic about what we can actually do for the next generation behind us. Let's trust they will continue to follow our examples.

AFFIRMATION: ***"I choose to see the good in all people. I positively contribute to a brighter future for humanity."***

MONTHLY MOONWORK:

- Brainstorm creative solutions to long-standing social issues you're passionate about.
- Take positive, peaceful action to assist the cultivation of a brighter future for the next generations.
- Choose your values and morals, then only make decisions that are in alignment with them.

♡ Fun, fresh, transformational products + services: https://choosebigchange.com ♡

Copyright © 2023 Tam Veilleux. All rights reserved worldwide.

FEBRUARY 24, 7:30 AM EST

FULL MOON AT 5° VIRGO

CHOOSE NON-JUDGMENT

Virgo thrives off order, routine, and control. When things get thrown off course, frustration ensues. But deep down, Virgo is always open to growing close with someone special, amplified by Venus square Jupiter this week.

You might find yourself suddenly aware of new opportunities for expansion within relationships. There are various preoccupations blocking your intentions, and it's easy enough to dislodge them with positive language.

Keep all words spoken aloud or within your head as uplifting as possible. Being rude and critical only results in complete shutdowns, and that's the opposite of what we want.

Virgo might not want to hear this, but being open and vulnerable is the *only* path to growth. Let go of your judgment habit, then watch all of your relationships transform.

This is especially true about your relationship with *you*. It is the *most* important relationship you will ever cultivate. All connections we make with others ultimately stem from there.

AFFIRMATION: ***"I am a compassionate communicator. I love myself!"***

MONTHLY MOONWORK:

- Actively work on being less judgmental, towards others *and* towards yourself.
- Be open to new ways of building intimacy within your relationships.
- Ensure all words you're speaking and thinking are uplifting, not draining.

Get your book bonus offers: www.choosebigchange.com/pages/bonus24

Copyright © 2023 Tam Veilleux. All rights reserved worldwide.

Numerology

February rolls in with its 2 blending with the 8 year to create a 1 energy, one of new beginnings (2 + 8 = 10, 1 + 0 = 1). We just had to work through a few things in January to make way for the new. Now you should have a clean slate by clearing out and planning transformation of things in your life that may have been weighing you down and holding you back.

Use that strong 1 energy this month to start the new things on your to do list. Stay focused and choose your tasks purposefully—there is a confidence and independence in this 1 energy that will help fuel your courage. We're in the beginning of the numerology energy cycle here and things will transform, grow and progress through the cycle in the upcoming months.

Aromatherapy & Gemstones

AROMAS: LAVENDER & CHAMOMILE Piscean, dreamy energy, is at the heart of this month's aromas of Lavender & Chamomile.

The benefits of lavender precede itself; it is widely used in the world of aromatherapy to promote relaxation and to counteract anxiety, depression, and fatigue. Chamomile is lavender's perfect sidekick. It, too, is known to soothe and relax while also boosting your immune system and provides anti-inflammatory responses. When combined together, this month's soothing combination wants you to relax your mind and see your dreams.

We live in a world where you can manifest and dream anything you dare to dream. Where does your mind go when it wanders? In order for us to go where the magic leads, we have to first be open to accessing it within ourselves. A relaxed state will help you access your magic.

GEMSTONE: AMETHYST Amethyst Crystals have long been synonymous with spirituality and healing. It is believed to enhance peace of mind, relaxation, self-discovery, courage and inner strength.

February provides you with an opportunity to activate your creative potential and to lean into your spiritual growth. As you set out to quiet your thoughts and relax your body it is important to create a space that will allow our intuitive insights to roll in. This month, leverage Amethyst Crystals to help you set the mood and bring purifying and clarifying energy into your space.

Your creative potential is boundless; Amethyst Crystals are here to support you in being the channel through which everything flows into existence.

ACCESS THE ENERGIES:

- Diffuse a blend of 3-4 drops of Lavender & Chamomile essential oils or apply to the bottom of your feet before bed.
- Hold a piece of Amethyst in your left hand or keep nearby during meditation to access your crown chakra.

♡ Fun, fresh, transformational products + services: https://choosebigchange.com ♡

Copyright © 2023 Tam Veilleux. All rights reserved worldwide.

The tarot card associated with Aquarius is **The Star**. This card is all about hope, inspiration, and renewal. It represents the ability to see the light at the end of the tunnel, even in the darkest of times. The Star encourages us to have faith in ourselves and in the universe, and to trust that everything will work out in the end.

In Aquarius season, you may be drawn to innovation and new ideas, and The Star encourages you to follow your unique path and trust your intuition. This card also represents healing and spiritual growth, reminding you to take care of your mind, body, and soul.

THE STAR AFFIRMATION ***"I am filled with inspiration and trust the authentic version of myself that shares my light with ease."***

Merry Meet!
The cold and dark still surrounds us, yet, we feel it. That hint of change, that glimmer of more light. It is Imbolc, the celebration of the mark of the coming warmth, of growth, fertility and hope. Our souls sing for it and we shall answer. We shall answer with meraki, the act of creating with complete passion and love. After all, February is a time for love also! So gather your tools and let's focus on our expanding and positive energies that are just waiting for you.

MERAKI EXPANSION RITUAL

A simple white candle represents all the elements. Oxygen for air, the flame for fire, the wax for earth, the warm melted wax for water. Carve a simple design into the earth of your candle (the wax) to represent your expanding energy. Use your fingernail as a personal tool, or carve with something that has meaning to you. Breathe over your carving then place your candle into a safe holder.

Voyage outside to collect symbols of the coming energy, pine cones and needles, rocks and branches, green from evergreens, for they hold all the magic of each season. Create a nest from your foraged items and settle your candle holder in the center.

You are now ready to bring the symbol of the coming light to life, strike the match and focus on the energy. Touch the flame to the wick.

Gaze, with soft eyes at the flame. Focus on thoughts of growing energy and light. Connect with these feelings. Should they wander, direct your thoughts back to positive energy. Stay until you feel the possibilities. Using your breath, darken the flame. Reconnect all month, as often as you need, to expand your spirit's energy.

Merry Part!

✯ Get your book bonus offers: www.choosebigchange.com/pages/bonus24 ✯

Copyright © 2023 Tam Veilleux. All rights reserved worldwide.

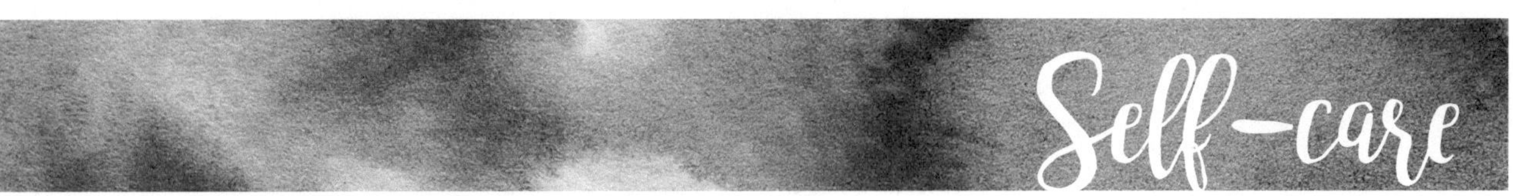

Leaning into the energy of risk-taking this month is much easier if you have a deep relationship with your intuition. Your ego screams at you like a drill sergeant while your intuition is quietly whispering messages that give you guidance beyond what your rational mind can comprehend. If you aren't used to following your intuition, these whispers can be hard to hear and come less frequently. As you develop this relationship, you will get stronger and more helpful messages that can make life so much easier. Learn how to connect with your intuition—go to the bonus page and follow the self-care link.

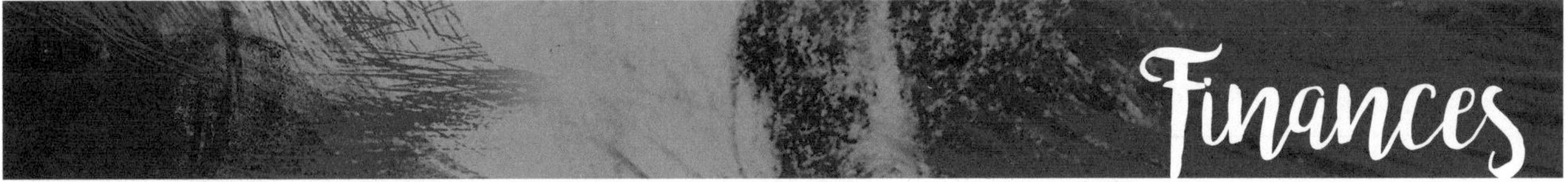

Now that you are more aware of what you think and say about money, I want you to be bold and lead the rebellion of your Parts. Your mind is like the mothership of your life, and she has to be heard, fed, and nurtured in order for you to grow into the insights that are fueling your future. Your Mother ship has many passengers. Those passengers are the Parts in your subconscious. Some Parts came on board when you were born, and other Parts developed as you grew. There's the infant, the eight-year-old, the rebel, the Parts of you that had certain experiences, etc.

In order to open the doors to more potential opportunities and expanded prosperity, you have to get in your subconscious and meet your money Parts. This is a great month for spiritual growth. How better to grow spiritually than to take the travel inside of you to meet those Parts?

Go to the Energy Almanac Bonus Page (www.choosebigchange.com/pages/bonus24), download your You're The One Journal and follow the link in the February section. I will take you on a guided visualization that specifically addresses your Parts. It will give you clarity on what your money directive is and then help you to visualize what you want your life to look like.

The month of love is upon us and did you know that, contrary to popular belief, the number one catalyst for laughter isn't a joke? People are more likely to laugh when they are interacting with another person; so take that as an opportunity to laugh with a friend, a partner, a colleague, a child, a stranger. The goal here is to laugh with someone else. This laughter exercise does include some physical touching so while I mentioned doing it with a stranger, it may feel rather awkward.

BACK HUG LAUGHTER

- For this laugh, you will either sit or stand with your back touching your partner's back and lock your elbows together.
- Then both of you start laughing.
- As you laugh, feel the laughter vibrating between your bodies.

Victor Borge once wrote, "Laughter is the closest distance between two people." This month you may feel some tension in wanting to do something more. Why not use this Back Hug Laughter as an opportunity to pause and reconnect to someone you love?

♡ Fun, fresh, transformational products + services: https://choosebigchange.com ♡

Copyright © 2023 Tam Veilleux. All rights reserved worldwide.

Copyright © 2023 Tam Veilleux. All rights reserved worldwide.

March

AN ABUNDANCE OF COMPASSION

MARCH 4 – 10

DO watch for confusion.
DO NOT compromise your standards.

MARCH 11 – 17

DO use discernment.
DO NOT be afraid to flow with change.

MARCH 18 – 24

DO demonstrate more love.
DO NOT dismiss the spring equinox.

MARCH 25 – 31

DO block time for deep reflection.
DO NOT fall prey to perfectionism.

IT IS SAFE FOR ME TO EXTEND COMPASSION TO MYSELF.

MARCH 10, 5:00 AM EDT

SUPER NEW MOON AT 20° PISCES

MAXED OUT DREAMS

MARCH 25, 3:00 AM EDT

FULL MOON LUNAR ECLIPSE AT 5° LIBRA

DISTURBING THE PEACE

♡ Love the Energy Almanac? Tag us on social media: @TheEnergyAlmanac ♡

Copyright © 2023 Tam Veilleux. All rights reserved worldwide.

March opens with the Sun tickling Jupiter in Taurus offering you hope about your personal worthiness as well as your personal resources. Keep reaching toward more light as you seek the early signs of spring. Taurus loves being in nature. Find a place where you can sink your feet into the mud while grounding in a vision of how to stabilize your material world.

On the 12th of March, Venus, the Marilyn Monroe of luminaries, will have moved into Pisces. She joins the Sun, Saturn, and Neptune making for an especially compassionate time period lasting through early April. Mid-month you may spend a few days lost in thought and visioning your future. Prayerfulness and journaling are good exercises for the 16th through the 18th after which you may consider ways to transform yourself and the greater group.

The planet of love and money, Venus, is going to skip around the cosmic playground at the end of March and she's teasing Jupiter into expanding our resources and self-worth before she goads Uranus about the same thing.

Spring suddenly seems surprising and delightful, doesn't it?

BOOK BONUSES INCLUDE DISCOUNT CODES, EBOOKS, SPECIAL REPORTS, AUDIO FILES AND SPECIAL OFFERS. TO GET ALL THE GOODIES, GO TO WWW.CHOOSEBIGCHANGE.COM/PAGES/BONUS24

KEY DATES

3/10	**New Moon in Pisces,** read moon article
3/11	**Mercury enters Aries**
3/12	**Venus enters Pisces**
3/16-18	**Sun in Pisces conjunct Neptune in Pisces**
3/19	**Spring Equinox**
3/21	**Happy Birthday, Aries**
3/23	**Mercury enters Pisces**
3/24-25	**Venus in Pisces sextile Jupiter in Taurus**
3/25	**Full Moon Penumbral Lunar Eclipse in Libra,** read moon article

Copyright © 2023 Tam Veilleux. All rights reserved worldwide.

MARCH PREDICTIONS

MONDAY, MARCH 4 – SUNDAY, MARCH 10

MOONS: SAGITTARIUS, CAPRICORN, AQUARIUS, PISCES

All eyes are on the economy both personally and globally this week. The third month of the year opens with soft and soulful communication teasing out ideas about the shifting economy when on Monday, Mercury sextiles Jupiter. Mid-week you can expect sudden revelations about resources, and on Friday and Saturday you could notice additional ideas and inspirations concerning the same topic. These thoughts blend equally with the urge to act on or express your frustrations about all of it (Mars square Uranus), perhaps finding you leading the charge for how money works or how value systems need to change. Employ compassionate viewpoints knowing that change is scary for many.

Sunday holds the gorgeous and spiritual new moon in Pisces where you can expect grand visions, uplifting dreams, and new creative endeavors to take shape. Be sure to read the moon article on that day.

GIFT & SHADOW THIS WEEK: *The gifts outweigh the shadows this week, which is a wonderful start to March. We are working through the energy of "allowing" with Jupiter, the great benefic, helping us to realize that we do not have to compromise our standards in order to realize our intentions. There is also a wonderful grace happening this week in terms of our emotional well-being. Maybe we are understanding more about how to use our emotions wisely instead of over reacting. We do have to watch out for confusion this week—especially if we are overly dependent upon our minds for answers. It's the heart baby! That's where the true North truly is.*

MONDAY, MARCH 11 – SUNDAY, MARCH 17

MOONS: ARIES, TAURUS, GEMINI, CANCER

This week, personal planet Mercury moves into the sign of Aries. This transit will last until early in May and involves a retrograde in April (warning Will Robinson!) When the depositor of communication is in the football uniform of warring Aries, you'd better watch your words. They are likely to fly out of your mouth before you can even rethink them, never mind retracting them. You're likely to speak what is on your mind, so if you can and when you can, pause before speaking. Venus, planet of relationships, peace keeping, and abundance enters the creative and spiritual sign of Pisces. Compassion and free flowing love are at an all-time high and relationships can deepen over the next three weeks. Are you seeking a soul mate? Now is the time! For March 12-15 enjoy the moon's lunations and lean toward nesting and food prep, a good book on a new subject, and using your intuition. At the end of the week, some grand vision is building and you could find yourself feeling a closer connection with Source and an expanded feeling of love. Watch the global front as well for a leader who may publicly share their own faith.

GIFT & SHADOW THIS WEEK: *Discernment is key this week. Our ability to know what is true and authentic for us as individuals far outweighs what we are conditioned to believe. Rather than allowing the outer world to cause you to doubt yourself, instead be more discerning with the information you are taking in and answer the question, "Does this feel right to me." Change is another topic of interest this week. Your emotions are the key to what is correct for you—they align you with your heart. Don't be afraid to go with the flow of change.*

Copyright © 2023 Tam Veilleux. All rights reserved worldwide.

MONDAY, MARCH 18 – SUNDAY, MARCH 24

MOONS: CANCER, LEO, VIRGO

Monday continues your enthusiasm for love while Thursday and Friday bring metamorphosis to mind once again. "How can I participate more fully in humanitarian efforts, innovation, and freedom?" Allow this to permeate you and jot down ideas that you can work with, remembering that you, too, are part of the collective soup. Your sense of loyalty, compassion and commitment to a spiritual practice or creative endeavor will be present as well.

When the spring equinox arrives on Wednesday, plan a social gathering and a reverent ritual to welcome the change. Read more about rituals by our writer, Kara. Let her suggestions lead the way toward a lighter, brighter spring, filled with intention.

The weekend finds Mars moving into Pisces. He joins Venus and Saturn for a romp through the Cosmos, or more likely, a slow stroll as Mars in this zodiac is slower and more thoughtful about how he behaves. Behaving more like a pacifist now, Mars will help you seek understanding and be more likely to respond rather than react. Also occurring this weekend is the tête-à-tête between Venus and Jupiter. This sextile brings an exciting opportunity for abundance and will last through Monday. Jupiter in Taurus amplifies resources and Venus in Pisces is creative and soul-filled. Perhaps you'll display your art, sing a duet publicly, or publish a collaborative book of prayers. The possibilities are endless, but if you're reading ahead, do bookmark this time period for special endeavors!

GIFT & SHADOW THIS WEEK: *As we move through the equinox this week, we are reminded that LOVE is the answer to all the questions. The Sun shows us the highest order of love—Universal Love. And as he crosses through the portal of the equinox, we are tasked with expressing that level of love in the physical 3D world. In fact, every seasonal shift brings us the opportunity to demonstrate more love on the planet. The only thing that can derail this passage for us is if we fail to love ourselves first. Love of Self = Love of Humanity, Love of Spirit, and Love of the Physical Body.*

MONDAY, MARCH 25 – SUNDAY, MARCH 31

MOONS: LIBRA, SCORPIO, SAGITTARIUS

As the cooler weather slides joyfully away and the smell of mud makes you smile, March 25th offers the first eclipse of the year in the well-balanced sign of Libra. This Full Moon Penumbral eclipse in the sign of Libra is full of beautiful possibilities—read more about it in our article further along in this month's pages. Venus is still sextile with Jupiter—read last week's article for a reminder about that energy. Our robust moon article on the topic of the penumbral eclipse will surely help you release what may be in the way of your best goal-getting. Eclipses are the best doormen—they open doors and close them. You will be exposed to change. Expect it and accept it.

When Thursday approaches, your intuition may download a new idea that could create a valuable change in how you think about yourself. Self-love is an important part of being in this world. Your self-worth often represents your net worth, so as this transit hits, block time to remind yourself how loveable you are.

GIFT & SHADOW THIS WEEK: *Beginning this week and for the next seven weeks, the Earth is triggering the potential for paralysis and fear in everyone. This week it is the fear of not being "perfect" that we are working through. Perfection is a phenomenon that only happens in the now. When we are overly future-oriented, we are anticipating not experiencing the truth of perfection. This can cause us to become overly critical, inappropriately analytical, and fearful of expressing ourselves in the world. The good news? If we allow ourselves to feel the fear and do it anyway, we can find joy at the other end of the experience.*

♡ Fun, fresh, transformational products + services: https://choosebigchange.com ♡

Copyright © 2023 Tam Veilleux. All rights reserved worldwide.

March Moons

MARCH 10, 5:00 AM EDT
SUPER NEW MOON AT 20° PISCES

MAXED OUT DREAMS

Only three months into 2024, we're experiencing one of the more dynamic new moons of the entire year. Pisces is starry-eyed and creative, always getting lost in the clouds. Dreamy vibes are strong now. I dare you to dream as big as you can because this super new moon is *here for it*.

All new moons are great for planting seeds that will grow long into the future. This particular Pisces super moon is dwelling in the land of dreams. There's never been more fertile soil in which to grow them.

Mars and Uranus are working together alongside Luna, intensifying the energy further. Confidence, courage, and innovation are just some of what you might experience. We're in the middle of the super new moon cycle—manifesting has never been easier.

Change is on the horizon—are you excited yet? It's happening quickly. Stubbornness will only cause unnecessary delays. Detach from society and embrace a more independent path if the status quo doesn't suit your dreams. This is your official permission slip to do so.

AFFIRMATION: ***"My biggest dreams are coming true now!"***

MONTHLY MOONWORK:

- Schedule time to daydream and really *get lost within it*. This helps you get in the right mindset for manifesting it.
- Open yourself up to new ways of doing and seeing things.
- Carve out your own path to follow, even if you're the very first one to go that way.

☆ Get your book bonus offers: www.choosebigchange.com/pages/bonus24 ☆
Copyright © 2023 Tam Veilleux. All rights reserved worldwide.

MARCH 25, 3:00 AM EDT

FULL MOON PENUMBRAL LUNAR ECLIPSE AT 5° LIBRA

DISTURBING THE PEACE

Libra loves indulging in all things beautiful and luxurious, while also heralding justice and compromise. There's a temptation to not "disturb the peace" right now. But trust me, that isn't true *peace*. It's repression.

Venus and Pluto square off on this day as well. This could cause tension between these two planets, adding to the energy of the Full Moon. Venus wants to fulfill the status quo while Pluto is pulling for a rebirth. Prepare for the peace to be disturbed.

Libra thrives in times of peace and compromise. Pluto's influence of power creates fundamental transformation. You may have to take an uncomfortable stance for a bit in order to improve the foundation.

Ruffling feathers isn't automatically a bad thing. Those who love us unconditionally will want us to be happy and fulfilled with the relationship. The feathers will always settle back down, so it's really no big deal in the end.

AFFIRMATION: *"My relationships are fulfilling, respectful, and help me grow."*

MONTHLY MOONWORK:

- Lovingly say what you need to say in order to improve the foundations of your relationships.
- Exercise compromise with your loved ones so everyone's needs are being met.
- Embrace what's uncomfortable and inconvenient; it fosters growth.

♡ Fun, fresh, transformational products + services: https://choosebigchange.com ♡

Copyright © 2023 Tam Veilleux. All rights reserved worldwide.

Numerology

March comes in with its creative 3 energy and combines with the strong year 8 energy to create the master number 11 (3 + 8 = 11). Eleven is the Master Intuitive number—so be aware and alert to your intuition this month. Too many times we don't trust our intuition. Sometimes it's too subtle and we stay too busy to hear it. Other times, it's loud and clear and we have too much doubt and don't trust it. This is the month to trust and follow your intuition! The 11 carries many energies, besides the intuition, it has the new beginning and independent energy of the 1—doubled! And they blend to create a stable 2, which is the secondary energy of the 11. The two is stable and balanced and likes peace. Follow your intuition to allow the flow into peaceful stability and balance. This energy is strong around partnerships—any type of partnership—be aware and open to that in your life this month. Focus on connection and nurturing.

Aromatherapy & Gemstones

AROMAS: GERANIUM & GRAPEFRUIT Spring's return of light brings with it the collective energy of awakening. In March we will use the aromas of Geranium & Grapefruit to call in abundance and beauty from a space of deep gratitude.

Geraniums bloom for us each spring. Their blossoms stand for beauty, purity, and gentle love. Geraniums ask that we release greediness and that we do not grasp for more than we need. To do so, we must be deeply rooted into our gratitude.

Grapefruit instantly uplifts our spirits, raises our energy, and awakens us to our innate abundance.

With Spring upon us, Geraniums & Grapefruit are here to remind you that it is time to awaken to the greater good and that all abundance rises from gratitude. You're ready to be uplifted, energized, and abundant. You're ready to rise and shine.

GEMSTONE: PERIDOT Turn to Peridot Crystals when you are weighted down by fears and toxic behaviors. These glimmering green crystals will lift you up but will not leave you out of balance. Peridot Crystals are well known to bring you love, healing, and growth.

This March, get clear on what your priorities are. What baggage do you need to stop carrying in order to lift yourself into a higher state of being? Peridot Crystals will stabilize your mental and emotional states while asking you to detox and to release what no longer serves you.

Green is the color of healing and growth and—if you let it—love will heal you. Let go of what no longer serves you.

ACCESS THE ENERGIES:

- Diffuse a blend of 3-4 drops of Geranium & Grapefruit essential oils each morning. Let the fragrance linger in your space and in your heart.
- Place your Peridot crystal in a communal space in your home such as the Living Room or Kitchen to encourage joy and harmony.

Copyright © 2023 Tam Veilleux. All rights reserved worldwide.

The Tarot card associated with Pisces is **The Moon**. The Moon is a card that represents intuition, mystery, and the subconscious. It is a card of emotional depth, creativity, and psychic ability. It encourages us to trust our instincts and listen to our inner voice.

In Pisces season, you may feel the need for introspection, spiritual growth, and healing. Things this season may not be as they seem, and it is advised to look beneath the surface to find the truth.

THE MOON AFFIRMATION ***"I am fully in tune with my inner knowing and trust the depths of my emotions as they guide me towards growth and wellness."***

Merry Meet! The earth loves to feel you, connect to you, loves to feel your bare feet upon the grass and soil. The wind longs to blow through your hair. The Sun waits to shine upon your skin. The moon yearns to glow in your eyes. Do you know this to be true? I hope you whispered a "yes." This is the season to begin your reconnection to nature following your winter hibernation.

We should all have a Cynefin, a place in nature that feels like home, where, deep in our bones, we feel its spirit and we know it is ours. For some, this is by water, others, deep in a forest glen. For still others, an open prairie where the curve of the earth bends towards the horizon. Do you know your Cynefin? The soul knows when you are there because your eyes find perfect beauty. Your ears fill with the magical sounds of feathered souls, of blowing wind, and of peace. Your breath is deep and you can almost taste the freshness.

And now, for the magic of touch, you shall earth with your place. Earth? Yes. Earth, or Earthing is about drawing the loving and electric power from earth up to you, through you, by touch. Earthing answers the call of connection.

EARTHING

Head to your Cynefin. If you are particularly fortunate, you will be able to walk there. On your feet wear something easy to remove. Once there, remove your shoes and step barefoot onto the earth. Stand still, close your eyes, breathe deep and slow. Stay still, let the earth radiate her electric energy to you. Open your eyes, perhaps, whisper your thoughts. Walk, slow, full-soled steps along the earth. Stay as long as you can. Do this as often as you can. No worries should your ground still be frozen or snow covered right now. You may draw upon Earthing as soon as the ground thaws. For now, investigate Earthing and its many healing powers and be ready. Merry Part!

♡ Fun, fresh, transformational products + services: https://choosebigchange.com ♡

Copyright © 2023 Tam Veilleux. All rights reserved worldwide.

Self-care

Worthiness is the number one reason most people don't practice self-care. The majority of people will blame it on not having enough time, but that is a nice excuse to cover up something you may not want to admit. The truth is that you don't see yourself as worthy so you leave yourself until last on the to-do list and never get around to it. This month I have a special Emotional Freedom Technique for you to clear these limiting beliefs of unworthiness from your body and mind. Go to the bonus page and follow the self-care link to check it out.

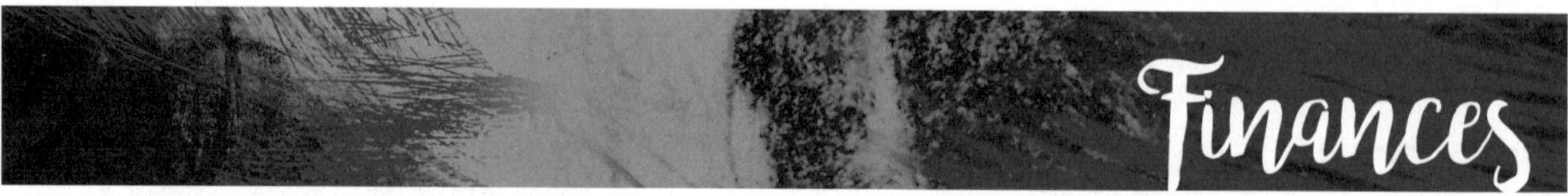

What a fabulous month to dive into your personal worthiness. I encourage you to be compassionate with yourself. In the last two months you have no doubt drudged up thoughts that were not all positive.

Begin to love all of those Parts within your SELF. I know it's not easy to love the negative or to even shine the light in there to see what's going on. What happens when you do though, is you discover your truths. When you discover your truths, you can transform your worthiness feelings into lighter and brighter Parts that then catapult you in the direction that you want.

Let's take it a little easier on your emotions this month. Today love every negative or positive thought that flows out of your mouth and what is in your mind. This will take practice and you may think it's silly, but it is important because this is the beginning of feeding and nurturing your mind. It's easy. You think something negative, you recognize it, then instantly, put your hand on your chest and love yourself. Your Parts only know what they know. When you start loving them, regardless of their portrayed negativity, they will begin to heal.

Pray, journal, and vision yourself grounded in love and knowledge that helps you feel stabilized in your world. Get this down and your life, money included, will expand exponentially!

FUN, FRESH, TRANSFORMATIONAL COMPANION PRODUCTS TO HELP MAKE 2024 AMAZING ARE AVAILABLE AT:

WWW.CHOOSEBIGCHANGE.COM

Copyright © 2023 Tam Veilleux. All rights reserved worldwide.

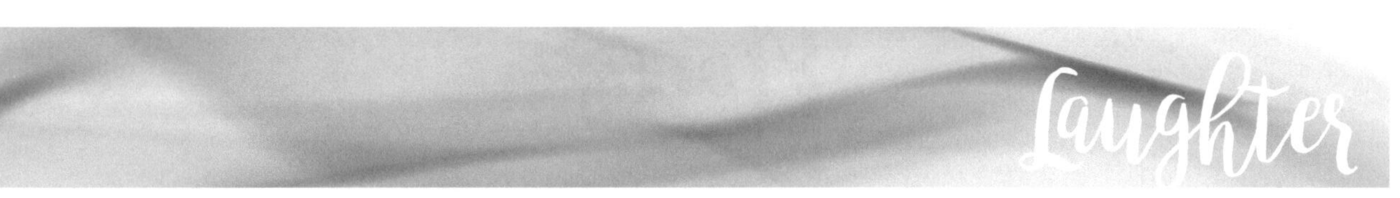

This month we celebrate the equinox and usually we move our clocks ahead an hour. If the Sunshine Protection Act goes through, we may not be changing our clocks this year but this is still a time of reflection and renewal.

This month our laugh is called **Time to Laugh** and like the equinox, where the Earth's equator on its axis passes the same plane of the sun's equator, we will pass through the equator of our body to test our balance.

We will start on one foot and test our balance. Don't worry, we will do this on both sides.

- Start standing on your dominant foot and then bring the other foot into the air a few inches.
- Move your foot like the hands of a clock starting at 12 o'clock all the way to 6 o'clock.
- As you move your foot around the clock, add a laugh for the number you are on, for instance: 1) Ha, 2) Ha-ha, 3) Hahaha, 4) Ha ha ha ha, 5) Haha haha ha, 6) Haha haha haha
- Then move your foot back up to the 12 o'clock spot going in reverse order.
- Then do the other foot.

Once you have completed both sides of **Time to Laugh** you may feel like you are more balanced, ready to take on whatever the month may send your way. Use this move every day this month or just when you are feeling off kilter.

LUMINOUS MOON DESIGN + PRESS
ASTROLOGY • TAROT • MANIFESTING • NUMEROLOGY

ORACLE CARDS THAT USE THE LANGUAGE OF ASTROLOGY 
HOUSE OF ASTROLOGY® ORACLE CARDS
THE FUNDAMENTALS OF ASTROLOGY
by Heather Arielle
A 52-CARD DECK & FULL-COLOR GUIDEBOOK
Artwork by Thom Cummins
Manifest your heart's desire with 52 beautifully illustrated cards that capture the nuance and duality of each zodiac sign, planet, and house. Use as oracle cards, for spreads, and to learn astrology.

COLOR YOUR OWN TAROT MAJOR ARCANA CARDS 
HOLY ORDER OF MANS
TAROT 22 KEYS
the Major Arcana
COLORING DECK
The Tarot Major Arcana represent the Path of Initiation and depict the workings of mind & soul on the Way of Enlightenment. Coloring the cards enables that awareness.

FIND PURPOSE AND PASSION THROUGH MANIFESTATION 
An Alignment of Spirit
FINDING WORK YOU LOVE
MICHELLE WALTERS
A guide to the inner work necessary for a successful career and all aspects of life using the Manifestation Wheel. Creative activities, manifesting & self-hypnosis.

COMPLETE YOUR NUMEROLOGY CHART 
Wisdom of Numerology
SUZAN OWENS
A concise guide to Numerology with quick number reference, definitions, calculations in a nutshell, and blank charts.

Available from Amazon, Barnes & Noble, and wherever books are sold.
Visit our website for more information and to discover more illuminating titles.
LUMINOUSMOON.COM

Copyright © 2023 Tam Veilleux. All rights reserved worldwide.

☆ Get your book bonus offers: www.choosebigchange.com/pages/bonus24 ☆

Copyright © 2023 Tam Veilleux. All rights reserved worldwide.

April

ANALYZING THE POTENTIALS

APRIL 1 – 7

DO address spiritual pursuits.
DO NOT compare yourself to others.

APRIL 8 – 14

DO work toward aligning with your spiritual nature.
DO NOT over complicate your world.

APRIL 15 – 21

DO expect incredible new insights.
DO NOT forget to ground yourself.

APRIL 22 – 28

DO celebrate through facing your fear.
DO NOT avoid doing transformational work.

IT'S SAFE FOR ME TO WAIT BEFORE TAKING ACTION.

APRIL 8, 2:21 PM EDT

NEW MOON SOLAR ECLIPSE AT 19° ARIES

COSMIC GREENHOUSE

APRIL 23, 7:49 PM EDT

FULL MOON AT 4° SCORPIO

EXPLORING BY MOONLIGHT

♡ Love the Energy Almanac? Tag us on social media: @TheEnergyAlmanac ♡

Copyright © 2023 Tam Veilleux. All rights reserved worldwide.

April is a time of great energy and, Little Pretzel, this month you might want to cool your jets and just enjoy the soft breezes that this month brings. Mercury is going to jump right into retrograde motion on the1st and take you on a nice slow ride until the 24th. It's the perfect month for considering and reworking how you do bold leadership. Use the first three weeks of the month for this work. While Mercury naps, Venus will step into Aries and suddenly sparks are flying and charisma is amplified. Remember! Though you may feel the urge toward action that creates transformation, you'll want to double-check and be sure what you're doing is right and smart. The retrograde in Aries whispers, "Don't start anything new." The middle of April brings a major aspect when Jupiter in Taurus conjuncts with Uranus in Taurus. The transit from April 15-26 brings innovation for working with resources and can inspire new technology, too. There is likely to be an impact on the economy.

BOOK BONUSES INCLUDE DISCOUNT CODES, EBOOKS, SPECIAL REPORTS, AUDIO FILES AND SPECIAL OFFERS. TO GET ALL THE GOODIES, GO TO
WWW.CHOOSEBIGCHANGE.COM/PAGES/BONUS24

KEY DATES

Mars in Pisces all month

4/1-24	**Mercury Retrograde in Aries**
4/6-7	**Venus enters Aries**
4/8	**New Moon Solar Eclipse in Aries,** read moon article
4/15-26	**Jupiter conjunct Uranus in Taurus (4/20 exact)**
4/20	**Happy Birthday, Taurus**
4/23	**Full Moon in Scorpio,** read moon article
4/25	**Mercury stations direct in Aries**
4/30	**Venus enters Taurus square Pluto**

Copyright © 2023 Tam Veilleux. All rights reserved worldwide.

APRIL PREDICTIONS

MONDAY, APRIL 1 – SUNDAY, APRIL 7

MOONS: CAPRICORN, AQUARIUS, PISCES

Warmer weather in the United States is a lovely way to begin the month along with Mercury going retrograde in the fiery sign of Aries. This slower period is your opportunity to cool your jets and do some deep thinking and reworking of plans before taking any action. It's actually a great opportunity to revisit your leadership style, too! Use the first three weeks of the month for this work. On Wednesday, Venus will conjunct Neptune and a sweet and soulful energy permeates the air, perhaps making it a grand day for prayer and meditation as both planets are in the sign of Pisces. A second option is leaning into your creative endeavors or spending time visioning the way you wish life to be. It's a green day, so go for it. The weekend has Venus entering Aries and for the next several weeks your charisma, and everyone else's, goes off the charts and there is a passion for leading, productivity and taking action. Flash your smile and grab the reins, Little Pretzel, your time for planning is now. No actions yet. The weekend holds a two-day transit of wondering how your own governance style, unique as it may be, might benefit the ongoing changes in humanitarianism and freedom.

GIFT & SHADOW THIS WEEK: *The shadow energies of control and inadequacy are what we are working on through this week. While we may be struggling with our need to control or being controlled by others, the truth this week is that we are only responsible for regulating ourselves. We cannot control everything and everyone around us, but if we relax and just take care of ourselves, so much more is possible! Inadequacy is the fear we deal with this week, which primarily is triggered when we compare ourselves to others. You are ENOUGH. Remember that this week and all will be well.*

MONDAY, APRIL 8 – SUNDAY, APRIL 14

MOONS: ARIES, TAURUS, GEMINI, CANCER

The second week in April starts with a New Moon Solar Eclipse in the sign of the ram. Leadership initiatives are available and passion is on high. Be thinking about your own style of administration. Is it dynamic enough? Read our moon article to dive deeper into this lunation. With the urge to take action, this is your reminder to hold off. Mercury is still retrograde. It's the moon in the sign of the ram that's nudging you. Sit on your hands if you must.

On Tuesday, Mars joins forces with Saturn until Sunday. They are in the same sign of Pisces, both urging you toward applied spiritual discipline. Don't miss the chance to tighten up your practices and employ more compassion. Saturn encourages proper timing and methodical planning—use the energy to discover what's missing. Perhaps do some more dreaming on these days. Expand your vision of what you can do to tighten up your faith or end martyrdom. When Saturday and Sunday arrive, your mind may be quite busy. The urge to "do" is there. Move if you must, but stay cognizant of the retrograde.

GIFT & SHADOW THIS WEEK: *Astrologically this is a complex week of energies that can trigger both fear and love (shadow & gift). The first gift of the week is simplicity! We have created rather complex lives and this week gives us the opportunity to drop into the simplest and most pleasant of the circumstances we are faced with. There may also be triggers in the outer world that make us a little fearful about the future. Truthfully, you are well-equipped to move with ease and grace through all life's experiences by staying "in-tune" with your intuition and instinct. Lastly, Neptune, the planet of unconditional love, moves into the Gate of Spirit initiating us into becoming more aligned with our higher selves. Circle this week on your calendars!*

Copyright © 2023 Tam Veilleux. All rights reserved worldwide.

MONDAY, APRIL 15 – SUNDAY, APRIL 21

MOONS: CANCER, LEO, VIRGO, LIBRA

This week holds some important information and it begins on Monday morning, lasting for 12 days. The effect of the transit will, however, last much longer. Jupiter, planet of expansion and optimism, will conjunct Uranus, planet of sudden insights. Both planets are in the sign of Taurus. Under this transit are great opportunities. Innovative ways of working with resources may reveal themselves. New technology for uses of energy or maybe new and inspiring discoveries in other areas will show up. This transit is landing at the same conjunction point as the May 2000 event, likely leaving an impact on monies and the economy. Jupiter expands and Taurus represents money which can, in turn, represent greed. Hold a vision for a positive outcome, but watch the economy to see how this lands. Remember, it's a 12-day event.

On Thursday, Mars in Pisces tickles Jupiter in Taurus, providing a spiritual flavor to your value system. Some grounding work would be appropriate as you vision opportunities you'd like to take that would expand your money. A walk in nature may help connect you to new ideas about self-worth, too. Your self-worth represents your net worth, this is no time for martyrdom or victimhood. Use the transit to break beliefs that aren't supporting you emotionally. This is a time for developing self-compassion.

Friday into Saturday is a weekend long cosmological rave dance party. To break down to basics, use Thursday through Sunday to work on your own personal transformation. Take actions that move you closer to self-love like visioning yourself successful, or in a relationship or maybe just seeing yourself fully happy. Expect to receive incredible new insights about how to use your expanding resources or how to shift your self-worth. It's basically a big weekend that you should block off for diligent application and use of the energies.

GIFT & SHADOW THIS WEEK: *What is success? What is failure? We may be struggling with these two energies this week. We all have ambitions, dreams, and goals, and how do you judge yourself in realizing those aspirations? If we are harsh in our judgment of success or failure, we may totally miss the lesson involved in the experience. Celebrate all your experiences as they are filled with truths that you wanted to learn.*

ENERGY ALMANAC CHALLENGE: Block off one hour a day Thursday through Sunday and take yourself through the process of "Who am I?" "Who do I want to be?" and "What belief is stopping me from reaching my fullest potential?" Make a social media post about this topic and tag us so we can honor your work. Saturn in Pisces...ya know? Well, when you know, you know.

♡ Fun, fresh, transformational products + services: https://choosebigchange.com ♡

Copyright © 2023 Tam Veilleux. All rights reserved worldwide.

MONDAY, APRIL 22 – SUNDAY, APRIL 28

MOONS: LIBRA, SCORPIO, SAGITTARIUS, CAPRICORN

With transformation still on your mind Monday morning, you might want to tread lightly. Considering the cosmic rave party of last weekend, you sure deserve a break! Tuesday's Full Moon in Scorpio can help you release whatever is in the way of your transformation. Read our moon article for ideas that will help heal those darker parts of yourself. On Thursday the planet of communication, Mercury, stations direct. Your quick wit and impetuous communication style could find you speaking too quickly again. Stay mindful of your urges to say what's on your mind and tamp it when you can. As the planet exits the retro-shade period next week, you'll likely feel it ramp up. It's a better time to take actions, sign contracts and agreements, but it's still not perfect.

On Sunday, Pluto begins a 3-day transit with Neptune. Mars and Neptune are both in Pisces. Pluto is in Aquarius. Under the Pluto-Neptune transit, expansive visions of a life of love and lolly-gagging are afoot. Notice an uplevel in compassion and emotion. Use the time to dream into your next best concept for your life. Get creative and also make a plan for activating the vision. Pray it up, write it out, then speak it out loud with emotion for best results. Do the work 3 days in a row as a grand way to exit April.

GIFT & SHADOW THIS WEEK: *Celebrate through releasing fear—Yay! We are nearing the end of the Earth's transit through the Gates of fear in our Human Designs. Most of all the fears would disappear if we were to do one thing first: practice self-care and self-love. Life really is an adventure and we are the drivers. When we make decisions that come from healthy self-centeredness, we find ourselves in the right place, at the right time, with the right opportunities. So enjoy life, face your fears, and celebrate moving ahead fearlessly!*

Copyright © 2023 Tam Veilleux. All rights reserved worldwide.

APRIL 8, 2:21 PM EDT
NEW MOON TOTAL SOLAR ECLIPSE AT 19° ARIES

COSMIC GREENHOUSE

Aries is that fiery, ambitious perfectionist filled with contagious passion! We're experiencing a roaring fire of energy right now during this Aries new moon *total solar eclipse*. Retrograde Mercury and Venus are also in Aries. The fire has been building for a few weeks now. Have you felt it? Have you added kindling to it?

This month's super new moon is much spicier than the rest of them this year. Luna in Aries loves a challenge, so it's a good thing we used last month's super new moon in Pisces to plant our huge dream seeds.

Imagine you planted your manifestation seeds in the most perfect cosmic greenhouse. Your job now is to give them water, fertilizer, and love.

Beware the temptation to speak all thoughts aloud unfiltered. Notice when your tough love may have gone a little too far. Is that the energy you want to bring into your cosmic greenhouse?

AFFIRMATION: ***"I love and embrace challenges. I overcome them with grace and ease."***

MONTHLY MOONWORK:

- Flip back to your monthly moonwork from February and March. Reflect on what has manifested from then till now, and how that can continue to grow or change from here.
- Put out your sacred tools on your windowsill or patio to soak up eclipse energy.
- Continue to practice meditation and mindfulness daily to stay grounded.

♡ Fun, fresh, transformational products + services: https://choosebigchange.com ♡

Copyright © 2023 Tam Veilleux. All rights reserved worldwide.

APRIL 23, 7:49 PM EDT

FULL MOON AT 4° SCORPIO

Scorpio loves the dark, peculiar side of life. While the full moon lights up the sky tonight, Scorpio may feel a little blindsided. But Luna only illuminates what needs to be released, so don't be afraid to let the moonlight in.

Saturn and Mercury are making this easy for us by clearing our heads and helping us reorganize things. Shuffle some stuff around. You'll definitely find a few things you can unburden yourself from.

Jupiter conjunct Uranus can bring unexpected surprises and opportunities from anywhere. Use that bright moonlight to explore exposed secrets. The dots will practically connect themselves once you dig deep enough.

Luckily, Scorpio *loves* to delve ever deeper. But we aren't just divers exploring the depths for fun. We're working towards growth and integration, so exploration has to be hands on.

The path is clear now (thanks to Saturn!) and we're being led down it. Continue to clear away what doesn't serve your highest good to make room for what does.

AFFIRMATION: ***"I am open to exploring my shadow self with love and acceptance"***

MONTHLY MOONWORK:

- Journal, journal, journal! Use up all the space you need while exploring your shadow self.
- Practice forgiveness and approach your depths with curiosity.
- Go at your own pace. There's no need to bite off more than you can chew.

Get your book bonus offers: www.choosebigchange.com/pages/bonus24

Copyright © 2023 Tam Veilleux. All rights reserved worldwide.

Numerology

April's 4 combines with the 8 year to create a 3 energy in April (4 + 8 = 12, 1 + 2 = 3). The three energies are very active, very creative and innovative. It's thinking out of the box energy. It's creating something new from the existing things and combining 2 things to make a new 3rd thing. It's about fertility and reproduction; not as much literal reproduction as it is giving birth to new ideas. The creative energy of the 3 has a very artistic energy, even if you don't think you're artistic, you may feel a little more creative this month. Amplify this energy by purposefully adding a little creative activity to your life in April. Use watercolors or enjoy the art of others, experience harmony while singing, dancing or just listening to music. Immerse yourself in something like this and notice your creative juices flowing.

Aromatherapy & Gemstones

AROMAS: JASMINE FLOWERS & SANDALWOOD While the energy of growth and newness abound, this month's fragrance encourages you to cultivate a space to nurture yourself before you move into the world. Using the soft scent of Jasmine Flowers & Sandalwood, take time to meet yourself in the quiet. Say "Hello" to your deepest voice and inner truth.

Sandalwood's fragrance is familiar and nostalgic, warm and romantic. Jasmine Flowers are soft and floral, sweet and sensitive. These white flowers harness their energy during the daytime and only bloom in the dark under the light of the moon.

There is nothing to fear from turning inwards this month. Simply use this time to tune into your deepest voice and inner truth. There is no forcing to be done; all you have to do is listen and welcome the presence of your inner truth. Like Jasmine Flowers who bloom only under the light of the moon, you too, must nurture and harness your energy until it is your time to shine.

GEMSTONE: AQUAMARINE April asks that we tap into our intuition and go with the flow. Aquamarine Crystals are blue-green glimmering stones which strengthen intuition, communication, and clarity. They encourage us to surrender and ride the wave!

As you move through this month, let Aquamarine Crystals cleanse you of your worries and refresh your perspective. Difficulties show up in our lives all the time. It is how we consistently respond to our challenges that matters most. When we feel like we are swimming upstream, we are in a space of resistance, anxiety and stress. Aquamarine Crystals invite you to welcome challenges with openness, acceptance, and positivity and watch your life return to its healthy and positive flow. Ride the wave!

ACCESS THE ENERGIES:

- Diffuse a blend of 3-4 drops of Jasmine & Sandalwood essential oils at the break of dawn or at dusk each day.
- Hold your Aquamarine in your left hand or keep nearby during meditation to access your throat chakra.

♡ Fun, fresh, transformational products + services: https://choosebigchange.com ♡

Copyright © 2023 Tam Veilleux. All rights reserved worldwide.

The Tarot card associated with Aries is **The Emperor**. The Emperor is a card that represents authority, structure, and discipline. It is a card of leadership, ambition, and achievement. It encourages us to take control of our lives and to set clear boundaries and goals. The Emperor can also represent organization and planning, and a focus on practicality and efficiency.

In Aries season, you may feel a need to assert yourself, to take action, and to establish order and stability in your life. This is a great time to set boundaries with yourself and others while you take actionable steps towards your goals.

THE EMPEROR AFFIRMATION ***"I set healthy and firm boundaries based on my goals while I take inspired action that supports my aligned and fulfilled life."***

Merry Meet! There is great energy growing. The earth is moving and birthing a new season, the Sun is spreading warmth. In ourselves we feel momentum. There is an urging, an unnamed expectation to match the wild birthing of this new season that is upon us. Just as nature sends us rain and wind, the basic elements of life, we yearn to match the energy.

How do we harness this wondrous wildness building and bring the energy in us? As with all growth and change, it starts with ataraxia, being in a state of blissful and serene calmness. For within serene calmness, we find our center and our beginnings. From there, we capture the energy. Let's cast a spell to guide our energy, an Ataraxia Spell.

ATARAXIA RITUAL

Find a spell jar, small or ornate, large or plain will do. Cleanse your jar by gently blowing breath into it. As the world is a circle of 3, do this 3 times. As you build your spell, focus on your personal ataraxia.

Add to your spell jar:

- Sea salt, to balance your emotions.
- Bayleaf, to enhance feelings of tranquility.
- Basil, to erase negativity.
- Cinnamon, to surround you with protection.
- Black tea, to build strength.

Create layers, or stir it all together, let your intuition guide you. Place your spell jar lid on. With a white candle, drip wax upon the edges to seal your spell jar. Hold your jar to your heart and breathe over the seal. Place your magic where you will see it often. Hold it close at every chance and let Ataraxia cast its spell. Merry part!

✯ Get your book bonus offers: www.choosebigchange.com/pages/bonus24 ✯

Copyright © 2023 Tam Veilleux. All rights reserved worldwide.

April is a month to pause, reflect, and enjoy. Allowing yourself to just be and not take action can be a challenge for most people. We live in a society where being busy is a status symbol and your worth can feel like it is directly related to your productivity levels. This month I want to encourage you to find moments of stillness and savor the present moment in all your activities. Be fully present in everything you do and turn your busy mind over to focusing on the task at hand and finding gratitude for the opportunity.

You are more privileged than you realize and there are other people in the world that would be envious of the life you have. Acknowledging this can help you shift from the mindset that you "have to" do something into the attitude that you "get to" do something. Even a mundane activity like brushing your teeth can be a special moment of loving your body with appreciation and gratitude if you are fully present. Not everyone has their teeth, not everyone has access to dental care, not everyone has running water. Be grateful.

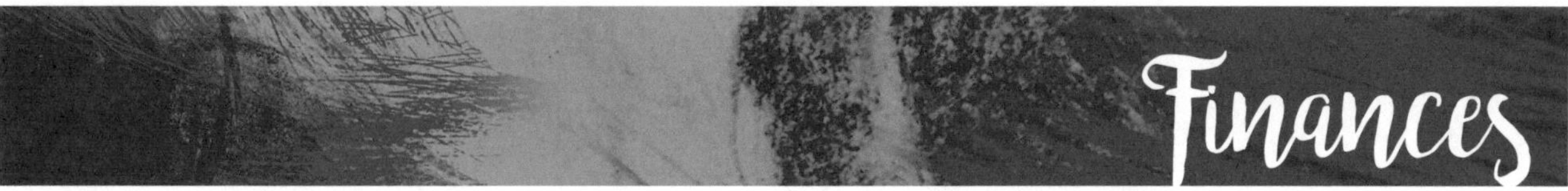

Nurturing your mind will awaken the sparks that ignite into the actions that create transformation in your daily life. The next step in your journey is to accept that it's ok that transformation takes time and that when you change your thoughts and behaviors, dissonance may occur. Perhaps you already experienced blocks popping up here and there that take you off track from focusing on you and your mind shifts. Breathe deeply into your abdomen and release the tension. It's ok that things don't work the way you want, really it is. Begin to love that part too.

An exercise to get your mind to awaken more is to take a look at what you are eating. You say, what does eating have to do with money? Everything! When you eat foods that put you to sleep, like carbs and sugar, your mind is not awake, it cannot focus, it is not alert and open. This is not about taking away; it is about enhancing. You, me, everyone is a work in progress. The question becomes: What makes me feel better, more energized, more awake? Then eat more of that. When you do, the other foods will organically not pull you towards them as much. But when they do, accept and love that side of yourself too. Relax my love, just relax into all of the Parts of who you are.

Go to the Energy Almanac Bonus Page (www.choosebigchange.com/pages/bonus24) to get your free You're The One Journal and you will receive a list of what I do to nurture and fill my mind, along with helpful hints on how to cut back on the foods that lull my mind, and maybe yours, too.

Copyright © 2023 Tam Veilleux. All rights reserved worldwide.

Because Mercury jumps into retrograde this month, it is a time to remember not to start anything new. But it is a perfect time to do some spring cleaning. Did you know that laughter reduces cortisol, which is a hormone that causes stress and increases endorphins which are the body's own natural opiates—they make you happy! According to the American Journal of Medical Sciences, when you laugh, the production of endorphins in your body keeps you feeling good for ages.

For this month, we are going to focus on getting rid of things that stress us and what doesn't stress us out more than emails in our inbox? **Delete Button Laughter** is a great way to quickly laugh your stress away.

For this activity, I want you to pretend you're sitting in front of your computer or maybe you're on your phone/ tablet and an email comes in. Just as soon as you see the email, you pretend to delete it and laugh. Keep going until you either feel the stress melt away from your body or your virtual inbox is clean.

Notes

Get your book bonus offers: www.choosebigchange.com/pages/bonus24

Copyright © 2023 Tam Veilleux. All rights reserved worldwide.

May

REVISITING THE PROSPEROUS VISION

APRIL 29 – MAY 5

DO take action toward your purposeful work.
DO NOT get caught up in dreaming.

MAY 6 – 12

DO seek solitude for realignment.
DO NOT share information at the wrong time.

MAY 13 – 19

DO trust in the abundance of the universe.
DO NOT avoid new opportunities.

MAY 20 – 26

DO wait long enough to know what is right for you.
DO NOT be overly generous this week.

MAY 27 – JUNE 2

DO use enthusiasm in a proactive way.
DO NOT avoid being social.

IT'S SAFE FOR ME TO EXPAND MY VISION OF PROSPERITY.

MAY 7, 11:23 PM, EDT

NEW MOON AT 18° TAURUS

GROUNDING IN CHANGE

MAY 23, 9:53 AM, EDT

FULL MOON AT 2° SAGITTARIUS

STAY THE COURSE

Copyright © 2023 Tam Veilleux. All rights reserved worldwide.

The month of May, which is every gardener's delight, holds some big movement and big growth if we all lean in. Early on you'll be glad to put your feet into the earth and ponder the changing landscape both figuratively and literally. Pluto, planet of regeneration, will retrograde in the sign of Aquarius and you get your first chance to see how freedom, innovation, and groups are shifting. This long retrograde will take you through the summer. Employ it wisely. Uranus will conjunct the Sun and your self-worth as well as your resources will be front and center, perhaps charging you with new insights that shift you but it's mid-month when things get exciting. The Sun, representing yourself and worldly leaders, will be busy chatting up Jupiter (beliefs and expansion) and Neptune (faith and visioning) all the while traipsing about with Pluto (regeneration) and Venus (love and money). When you stir up those cosmic ingredients, you end with a buffet of ideas concerning visions of expansive resources, bold leadership, and witty new ways of addressing change. Watch the dates between May 18th through the 24th for bubbling energy that you'll want to capture. Have plenty of journal space at the ready. When the month closes, the focus turns to education and learning as ideas about how we instruct begin their own journey of change. As the seeds you plant this month in your estate grow roots then sprout, so will the ideas that you spend time with in May. And hey, Little Pretzel, don't forget your sunblock, things are looking bright.

BOOK BONUSES INCLUDE DISCOUNT CODES, EBOOKS, SPECIAL REPORTS, AUDIO FILES AND SPECIAL OFFERS. TO GET ALL THE GOODIES, GO TO
WWW.CHOOSEBIGCHANGE.COM/PAGES/BONUS24

KEY DATES

5/1	**Mars enters Aries**
5/2	**Pluto retrograde in Aquarius**
5/7	**New Moon in Taurus,** read moon article
5/15	**A week to watch**
5/16	**Mercury enters Taurus**
5/21	**Happy Birthday, Gemini**
5/23	**Full Moon in Sagittarius,** read moon article
5/24	**Venus enters Gemini**
5/26	**Jupiter enters Gemini**

♡ Fun, fresh, transformational products + services: https://choosebigchange.com ♡

Copyright © 2023 Tam Veilleux. All rights reserved worldwide.

MAY PREDICTIONS

MONDAY, APRIL 29 – SUNDAY, MAY 5

MOONS: CAPRICORN, AQUARIUS, PISCES, ARIES

Monday begins the winding down of April and it's a continuation of the dreamy Pluto-Neptune transit. It's your continued chance to feel into transformation and use your currently ramped up intuition for moving into the future. Mars, the planet of action, is also active in the sign of Aries and wants you to take actions to initiate the end result. If it feels right, do it! Don't get caught dreaming but not doing. Wednesday finds Venus moving into Taurus and your senses are amplified. Being fully immersed in spring weather under this aspect gives you the chance to get outside and put your feet in the soil as you tend the garden and consider your profits as well as all things beautiful. If you experience some tense moments, blame Pluto who is tugging you toward your own transformation as it contributes to the bigger picture. Who must you become to fulfill your own potential? Is your self-worth in question? As you pull the weeds from the flower beds, pull the old stories from your psyche as a first step toward change. With Mars stimulating Pluto at the week's end, you'll surely be ready to act on needed changes.

Of key importance this week is Pluto's retrograde in the sign of Aquarius. For four months we've been addressing the good of the group and how we can transform freedom, innovation, technology, and humanitarian issues. When Pluto slows his powerful roll to a dull roar you can employ questions like, "How easy can it be to use technology for the good of the group?" Or, "What would it be like to employ intuition over what we're being told?" "How can change be easy and fun?" "What benefits can we gain by all of society being fed and sheltered?"

GIFT & SHADOW THIS WEEK: *This week's energy brings purpose, allowing, and fulfillment into focus. Purpose is tricky because we can fall into a trap of constantly seeking our purpose and potentially feeling like a failure if we don't find it or live it out. Instead, realize that when you are following your passion, your life is then a blank canvas and you're the artist. The art of allowing is built on trust and faith in your worthiness to have help along the way. We learn that no one is an island and that we all need each other in reaching the highest states of abundance, love, and support.*

MONDAY, MAY 6 – SUNDAY, MAY 12

MOONS: ARIES, TAURUS, GEMINI, CANCER

Welcome to the second week of May. On Monday and Tuesday, the Sun and Saturn are playing nicely in the cosmos, tickling your sense of spirituality. The need to take responsibility or seek solitude for the sake of realignment with Source will be active. Wednesday's New Moon in the sign of Taurus has your optimism, hope, and worthiness buoyed as well as, potentially, your bank account. Take the opportunity to address these topics under this earthy lunation. A ritual with flowers and food could be special. On Sunday you, or a world leader, may realize a sudden shift about resources. Uranus triggers change and involves a sense of revelation. You may intuitively know something of importance concerning your personal wealth or value system. On the global landscape, the economy may be repositioning.

GIFT & SHADOW THIS WEEK: *We all want to be heard, seen, valued, and recognized for our genius, but often we end up sharing information in the wrong timing and people look at us as if we have sprouted two heads! This week's gift is about you sharing your brilliance in the right time, with the right people. That means learning when it is appropriate to share and when it isn't. When is it appropriate? It is appropriate when you have been invited to share your insights. Slow down the process of sharing long enough to know whether what you have to say will be valued by those who hear your words.*

☆ Get your book bonus offers: www.choosebigchange.com/pages/bonus24 ☆

Copyright © 2023 Tam Veilleux. All rights reserved worldwide.

MONDAY, MAY 13 – SUNDAY, MAY 19

MOONS: CANCER, VIRGO, LIBRA, SCORPIO

This week ushers in two weeks of powerful astrological moves. The planets have a plan and your work, Little Pretzel, is to move with the energies. Read on to see what's ahead because many aspects involve you, represented by the Sun. The Sun in mundane astrology also represents leaders. As you read what's coming, think both personally and globally.

Monday opens with the Sun and Uranus still dancing together. If on Sunday you were getting sudden insights about resources, those ideas may still be present and they are melding with Venus and Saturn. Think: new ways with money as well as grounding in your sacred responsibilities. There may be a desire to shape a new outdoor altar or clean the one in your bedroom. Maybe you'll buy a new oracle deck or start saving for one before the last hurrah of Jupiter in Taurus hits you on May 17-19; this is just in time for an amazing and abundant weekend. Hear us out!

Friday begins the Sun-Jupiter conjunction. Sun is you; Jupiter is your faith and a sense of magnification. Sun is in Taurus as is Jupiter. This abundance trigger point is yours for the taking. Possibilities are everywhere if you are willing to believe it. Don't stay home, Little Pretzel, it's a day of adventure and you should plan a little foray on Saturday or Sunday. Meet people, share your bright light, and see what crops up for you. Sunday is a five-star day when Neptune joins the cosmic party adding a touch of soulfulness and a grand opportunity to create an expansive vision for your life.

Jupiter sextile Neptune is a 10-day transit worth its weight in gold. Jupiter is the wise, kind, mentor who cheers you on to your greatest potential. Currently, Jupiter is in the earthy, stable sign of Taurus, doing his work to give you hope about your finances and your own worthiness. Neptune, the spiritual guru, is engaged with Pisces, the creative. These two planets are holding hands and skipping across the cosmos and it's oh so pretty for you. Notice as you are offered by the universe, circumstances to increase your wealth or your self-worth. Pay attention to opportunities that expand how you think or feel about the economy and note that it has a deeply spiritual or sacred nature. Your imagination could be wildly expansive as you experience new dreams for yourself. There is a literal buffet available to you and it's flowing toward you. Reach out and grab some. Pray it up, say it up, and journal into your abundant new life.

GIFT & SHADOW THIS WEEK: *Money and abundance are the issues we must work through this week. Fear and worry about resources or having "enough" can be the source of our compromising ourselves. We are designed to have everything we desire and this demands that we trust in the abundant nature of the Universe and then align ourselves emotionally with being worthy of receiving. The high side this week is bounteousness, and in the low we have compromised what we love and want for we feel we have no choice but to settle.*

ENERGY ALMANAC CHALLENGE: Block this weekend off and create a brand spanking new vision board all about abundance. Take a picture of it and post it to social media. Tag us with @TheEnergyAlmanac and tell us your dream so we can write a wish with your name on it!

Copyright © 2023 Tam Veilleux. All rights reserved worldwide.

MONDAY, MAY 20 – SUNDAY, MAY 26

MOONS: LIBRA, SCORPIO, SAGITTARIUS, CAPRICORN

If you're reading ahead, mark this week in pink (only because we at the Energy Almanac office love pink). The astrology shows such incredible aspects, offering an abundance of opportunities starting with Monday and Tuesday. The Sun's last day in Taurus still has him enjoying time with Neptune and Jupiter. This holdover from the weekend gives you one more chance to revel in a vision of soulful abundance for yourself. Really sink into that dream. On Wednesday, you may be thinking about change. Be asking yourself questions. "Who do I need to be to innovate me?" Venus is still in Taurus and is encouraging Jupiter and Neptune to the dance. It's a divine time for grounding in your visions, feeling hopeful about your money and doing all of it with a dash of sacred alignment. Your heart will be filled with compassion so be mindful to not be overly generous to the point that you put yourself in a bad position because "the Lord helps those who help themselves," right? Greed or an over-generous spirit are some shadows to be concerned with. Also worth mentioning is the chance that you may be caught daydreaming a bit more often than normal. Ground yourself often under this transit.

As 2024 goes, our opinion is that the May 23rd Full Moon in Sagittarius is your best lunation for doing some big work around what you believe you can have. With the other planets mentioned above doing their work to help you understand that you can have it all, use the Moon energies to do the releasing of old, stuck stories. EFT anyone? If you don't know about Emotional Freedom Technique as a way to get unstuck, go to YouTube and find a practitioner. If you like our style, go to: www.youtube.com/TamIAmVeilleux for some videos on the topic.

Friday through Sunday, the Jupiter-Neptune transit is still active. Reread the paragraph from last week so that you use every spare minute enjoying the energies. On Saturday, Venus newly in the sign of Gemini could have you curious about technology, or freedom. Play with new ideas or start a juicy conversation with a partner about what transformations could benefit this area. Lastly, a major shift begins on Sunday as Jupiter enters the sign of Gemini for a 12-month stay. Read more about this transit in the front matter of this Energy Almanac. Watch for a growing curiosity and all eyes on the education system.

GIFT & SHADOW THIS WEEK: *Patience is a virtue, right? This week we have the temptation to jump and leap into and out of things without waiting, which can become problematic. This is a high energy week, but we can discover once it's over that we have over-committed ourselves to the wrong things. Instead be sure to wait long enough to know what is right for you and then choose your next steps. Otherwise, you may find that when what you truly desire comes along, you simply don't have the time or space to participate. PS: If you don't have that "knowing" of what is correct, then it's best to wait.*

FUN, FRESH, TRANSFORMATIONAL COMPANION PRODUCTS TO HELP MAKE 2024 AMAZING ARE AVAILABLE AT:

WWW.CHOOSEBIGCHANGE.COM

Copyright © 2023 Tam Veilleux. All rights reserved worldwide.

MONDAY, MAY 27 – SUNDAY, JUNE 2

MOONS: CAPRICORN, AQUARIUS, PISCES, ARIES

As May stretches into June this week, you still have time to dwell in possibility, but now there's a new flavor to it. Jupiter has changed its zodiac and is now in Gemini. Under the Jupiter-Neptune (curiosity-faith) transit, your thoughts are more in the form of questions. Gemini is the sign of the hungry student and you'll be more curious than ever.

For Monday and Tuesday this week, you'll be wondering how to apply spirituality to your own life. The window closes down on the 28th. Hopefully your dream board, vision journal, and plans for prosperity are firmly planted now and you'll find answers to your questions about realizing everything you've dreamed into. Tuesday brings the perfect time to compute and make practical plans relative to the ideas you've collected over the last ten days. Employ discipline and take responsibility by bringing order to the dream. On Thursday, Jupiter in Gemini enjoys time in the cosmic sandbox with Pluto, planet of power. Big questions fill you. "How can I be part of global transformation?" "How easy can it be to regenerate myself for the greater good?" "What part does learning have to do with change?" "What do I need to learn now?" Remember, ask good questions, get good results. And with Uranus and Mercury involved with the astro-dance on Friday, you can expect some sudden insights to all of that. Once again, Little Pretzel, have your pencil sharpened and notebook in hand.

The weekend is a great time to be social or take a short trip. You'll find your wit quick and your inquisitive nature burning for answers over the next week when the Sun conjuncts Venus until the 7th. Jupiter and Pluto are also present, expanding ideas about how we learn and how we can change education so that everyone can participate fully and more enjoyably. Gemini also rules information, short-distance travel and social engagement. There's much on the table for rebirthing.

Speaking of wit. Don't forget Sunday. Two nuggets of information for you. First, it's National Donut Day—grab yourself your favorite donut and raise a glass of milk or coffee. Second, celebrate our laughter articles. Everyone needs more laughter and the Energy Almanac series really nails it. Seriously, donut lettuce hold you back from a good belly laugh. Go to the bonus page to get more laughter ideas.

GIFT & SHADOW THIS WEEK: *Last week's focus on patience gets drawn out a little bit by Jupiter's move into the same energy. We have a chance to hone our skills in making decisions that are correct for us versus doing a lot of needless leaping in and out of commitments. There is something truly empowering this week, when we are able to use enthusiasm in a proactive way. That means choosing our paths deliberately based on whether we are truly excited by an opportunity or just momentarily enthused. You will be glad you entered into the right things for you!*

MORE BELLY LAUGHS & OTHER COOL STUFF!

Copyright © 2023 Tam Veilleux. All rights reserved worldwide.

MAY 7, 11:23 PM EDT
NEW MOON AT 18° TAURUS

Taurus is grounded, practical, and determined. All those big dreams have never seemed so possible! The recent streak of four super moons (including one eclipse) is over now. But Taurus still carries lots of manifesting potential if you wield it properly.

After all of those intense manifesting energies, Taurus is here to ensure all the work gets done through heightened dedication. It will lovingly play devil's advocate when things derail.

Abundance is quickly expanding in our lives now. All manifestations have the potential to bring us unbounded prosperity. We're getting a taste of that as Jupiter moves through Taurus.

Over the next few weeks, our thoughts are going through a revolution. Sudden change is intimidating, and Taurus is stubborn.

Grounding is very important to keep your energy clear and strong. Earthy Taurus needs a spiritual connection to nature in order to thrive. Go out under the dark skies or during the daylight hours and allow inspiration to flow.

AFFIRMATION: *"I am ready for changes. I handle big changes with grace."*

MONTHLY MOONWORK:

- Stay focused on your *big* dreams, and keep distractions to a minimum.
- Spend time outside, or at least breathing in the fresh air, to ground your energy.
- Find stability while riding the waves of change by grounding your energy through consistent meditation.

✯ Get your book bonus offers: www.choosebigchange.com/pages/bonus24 ✯

Copyright © 2023 Tam Veilleux. All rights reserved worldwide.

MAY 23, 9:52 AM EDT

FULL MOON AT 2° SAGITTARIUS

STAY THE COURSE

Sagittarius values freedom, fun, and independence. Sometimes independence looks like the ability to change personality traits on a whim. Our communication right now is quick, pointed, witty, and straight to the point.

Mars is filling us with jitters right now. Sagittarius already has a hard time sitting still. We may experience an overwhelming urge to take off running in any direction, just for the sake of movement. However, moving *around* doesn't automatically mean you're moving *forward*.

Before you accidentally leap into an abyss, take *several* deep breaths. Get back in touch with your strengths and get rid of whatever is blocking your way to them.

The cosmos are burning with creative ideas and optimism. Pick through them to find the ones that align *perfectly* with the intentions of the big dream seeds you've planted. Instead of starting an entirely new path, go *further* down the one you're already on. Sagittarius will love that!

AFFIRMATION: ***"All my words and actions are in alignment with the future I want to manifest."***

MONTHLY MOONWORK:

- Stubbornly stick with what's working. See it all the way through to the end before moving on.
- Banish limiting beliefs and self-deprecating habits that are muffling your strengths and passions.
- Get as physically active as you're able to get out all the jitters!

♡ Fun, fresh, transformational products + services: https://choosebigchange.com ♡

Copyright © 2023 Tam Veilleux. All rights reserved worldwide.

Numerology

The May 5 carries a very high energy that likes change, but when blended with the 8 year energy for manifesting, it creates a solid 4 energy (8 + 5 = 13, 1 + 3 = 4). The month energy wants to come in strong and fast—but that 4 is putting on the brakes. It's a safe energy and it's reminding us, after that busy creative energy of April, to take a minute to evaluate what we're creating and what direction we're heading. It's just a reminder for us to always take a pause and evaluate our goals and projects. The solid energy of the 4 likes strength, balance and stability. You must have a strong, stable foundation in order for anything to be built upon it if you want it to last. Take some time this month to evaluate your life, goals, and projects, and be certain that everything is going smoothly and is on the right path.

Aromatherapy & Gemstones

AROMAS: DAHLIA PETALS & LEMON ZEST This month we are spending time tending to our internal gardens. May's aromas are Dahlia Petals & Lemon Zest. They are a sweet invitation to take a stroll in a flower field and reminisce.

Dahlia flowers are a symbol of positivity, kindness, and love as these flowers will support you in embracing change. Lemon Zest is bright, familiar, and uplifting. These sweet, warm aromas create a positive atmosphere.

May's fragrance is designed to spark your memory by reminding you of simple, soulful, sunny times to bring you back home within. Take this month to feed your soul with flowers, friends and family because it is the seeds you plant today that will become the flowers that bloom tomorrow.

GEMSTONE: ROSE QUARTZ Rose Quartz is a rosy pink stone that supports us in communicating love and compassion.

May slides in with hopeful energy along with ideas and visions for change. Let us plant seeds of love and compassion for both ourselves and the collective this month by harnessing the heart-centered energy of Rose Quartz.

Planting seeds of self-love and compassion is a practice that requires you to heal emotional wounds and to call in love. With repetition, over time, your thoughts, words, and actions will align to create more positive and loving energy. With the support of Rose Quartz, everything in your life moves to a higher plane of vibration that is deeply rooted in love.

ACCESS THE ENERGIES:

- Nothing beats the aroma of fresh cut locally grown Dahlia flowers placed atop your window sill or centrally located in your space to brighten your room and your mood.
- Diffuse 3-4 drops of Lemon essential oil or place a few drops in your hands. Cup your palms at your face and nose. Breathe deeply for a positive, uplifting boost of energy.
- Hold a piece of Rose Quartz to your chest or keep nearby during meditation to access your heart chakra.

✯ Get your book bonus offers: www.choosebigchange.com/pages/bonus24 ✯

Copyright © 2023 Tam Veilleux. All rights reserved worldwide.

The Tarot card associated with Taurus is **The Hierophant**. The Hierophant is a card that represents tradition, structure, and spiritual guidance. It is a card of wisdom, knowledge, and mentorship. It encourages us to seek higher truths and to connect with our spiritual beliefs and practices. The Hierophant can also suggest a pull towards conformity, conservatism, and adherence to social norms.

In Taurus season, you may feel a need for guidance, support, and education, as well as a need to honor tradition and cultural values. Taking note of the relationship between self and others and whether or not they are supporting or adding value to your life will help during this season.

THE HIEROPHANT AFFIRMATION ***"I am rooted in my values and connect openly with new ideas and practices that support my health and growth."***

Merry Meet! Well, it is true, April showers bring May flowers. As the Sun thaws the earth, we are drawn more and more to delight in the bounds of what Mother Earth brings. We know the earth delights in our care and our touch, and so we shall indulge her! It is time to plant! Do not say you do not have a green thumb, for flower gardens take but simple care. Water, Sun and the most important element, admiration. While sun-shining flowers are grand, we must not be blind to the magic of moon-glowing flowers. This is where our May energy will go.

MOON GARDEN

A Moon Garden is a dark and quiet spot, where white flowers mimic the round full moon. Where fragrant scents fill the night air. Where magic is part of the beauty. Your moon garden may be hidden, perhaps, behind a hedge, where the moon beams will just peek at the flowers. Mayhap, it is the center of your garden, dancing in full moon light with a row of mismatched pots across your walkway, where its magic is on full view. The choice is intuitive, and, sometimes, just plain practical.

Your moon garden shall be brimming with white flowers and sweet nocturnal scents that will draw you close. Seek out white and fragrant flowers at your plant nursery. Did you know they are called plant nurseries as that is where you will find your plant babies? Choose enough to fill your moon garden.

GLOAMING RITUAL

Gloaming is that space of time between sunset and twilight. When the magic hour of gloaming arrives, begin to sow your moon-like babies. Watch how the light makes them glow. Add other magical elements, stones, twinkling solar lights, gazing balls, white flags and wind chimes. Create a stepway and a small place to sit in the middle. Circle your moon garden with a hand sprinkled ring of salt, to add protection for those night creatures that choose it as home.

Each gloaming, stroll to your moon garden. Carry your crystals and other magical tools for your rituals. Follow the moon guidance to open up the magical possibilities of your moon garden. Merry part!

♡ Fun, fresh, transformational products + services: https://choosebigchange.com ♡

Copyright © 2023 Tam Veilleux. All rights reserved worldwide.

April showers bring May flowers and I hope you are taking the time to appreciate all the new beauty that surrounds you. This is a great time to focus on self-care practices like grounding, earthing, forest baths, and taking walks in nature and gardens. Getting your skin in contact with the ground can be extremely beneficial for your stress levels, will decrease headaches, help you heal faster, and increase your energy levels. Grab the link on the bonus page for four simple grounding practices to help you find a way to get these benefits in a way that resonates with you!

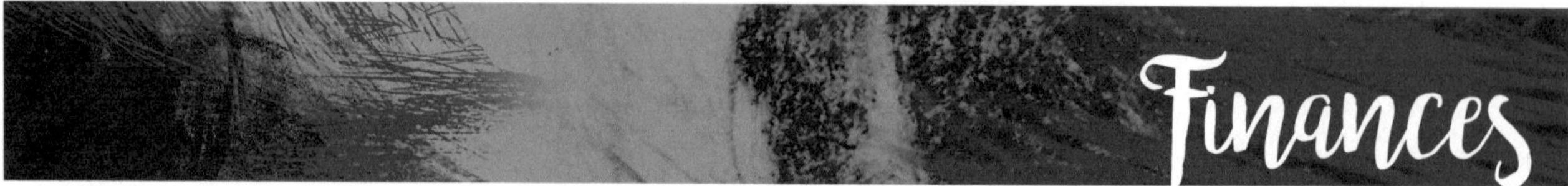

Spring is finally here! Let's get down to business then, it's education and learning month. Yay! I love to learn, don't you?

There are many rules about money—most are the hard-core, read a book, take a class sort of educational types. I will share those with you; however, for the energies of May, I want you to shift into a soft focus that regenerates your mind. Use your You're The One Journal to capture your ideas around:

- Love and money; how does that work out in your relationships? Is someone else controlling you and your money, or are you in control of your own money?
- Faith; does your belief system have reservations around being abundant?
- Self-worth; is it still wavering on the money front?
- Freedom; does money symbolize freedom for you? If not, what does it symbolize for you?

There is big movement this month and you can get on board with new insights that will shift you. As you are contemplating and journaling, don't forget to check in with your Parts and ask them what their answers are to any of the above questions.

Go to the Energy Almanac Bonus Page (www.choosebigchange.com/pages/bonus24) to get your free You're The One Journal and discover some of the hard-core ways that money works.

I think we have all heard the expression "April showers bring May flowers" and this still holds true today because April is historically a rainy month. The poem as we know it today originated all the way back in 1157, in the form of a short poem written by Thomas Tusser. The poem can be found in the April section of a collection of his writings titled, *A Hundred Good Points of Husbandry.* The poem goes as follows: "Sweet April showers, Do spring May flowers."

And since May is a time of renewal and new flowers blooming, it is the perfect time to stop and smell the flowers. This month, our laughter exercise is called **Flower Laughter**.

For this exercise, I invite you to stand up. Now act as though you are picking flowers from the ground or from a bush or a tree. As you stand up/sit up, bring the flowers to your nose and inhale. As you exhale, let out a laugh. Keep laughing until all of the breath is gone from your lungs. Then do it all again!

Copyright © 2023 Tam Veilleux. All rights reserved worldwide.

Notes

Copyright © 2023 Tam Veilleux. All rights reserved worldwide.

Get your book bonus offers: www.choosebigchange.com/pages/bonus24

Copyright © 2023 Tam Veilleux. All rights reserved worldwide.

June

NURTURING NEW IDEAS

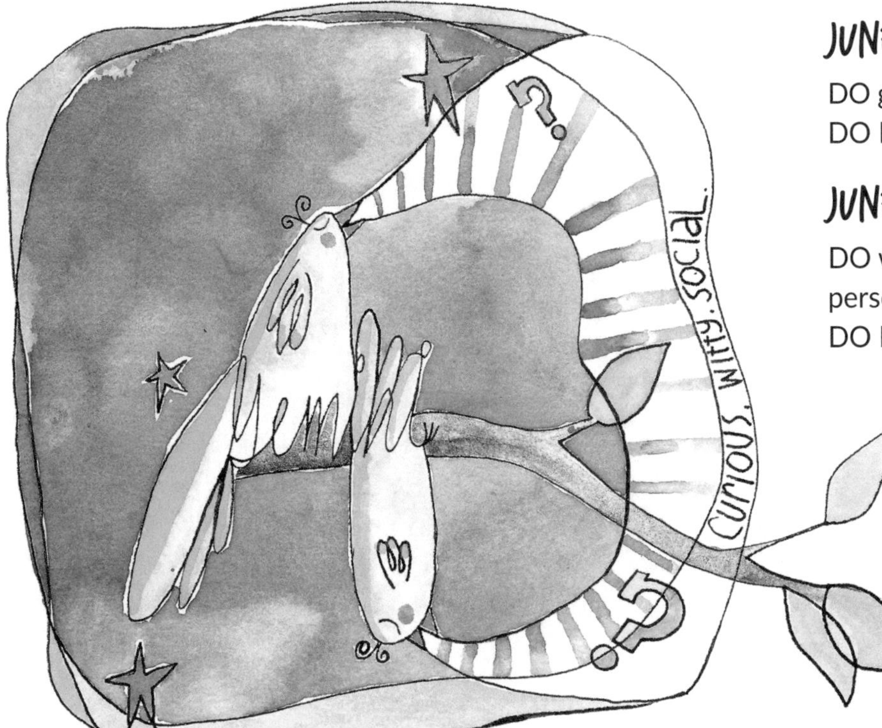

JUNE 3 – 9

DO gather information concerning your goals.
DO NOT be confrontational.

JUNE 10 – 16

DO work with and understand your own personal values.
DO NOT do something just to make money.

JUNE 17 – 23

DO focus on what's right.
DO NOT fall prey to unworthiness.

JUNE 24 – 30

DO honor yourself with kind thoughts.
DO NOT avoid relaxation and self-care.

IT'S SAFE FOR ME TO ENTERTAIN NEW IDEAS.

JUNE 6, 8:38 AM EDT

NEW MOON AT 16° GEMINI

HAVE MORE FUN

JUNE 21, 9:08 PM EDT

FULL MOON AT 1° CAPRICORN

RESPECTFUL DREAM CHASING

Copyright © 2023 Tam Veilleux. All rights reserved worldwide.

June

As school lets out in the northern hemisphere and our children make a collective sigh of relief, many adults will feel the pull to address the adjustments needed to make education better, smarter, more robust, fair, and inclusive. Top of mind is the education system and over the next many months as Jupiter tours the zodiac of Gemini, you can expect innovation in this area as well as short-term travel, information in general, and how much you socialize. Later in June, you could find yourself analyzing relationships and the household budget. There are some new concepts trying to form, but there's tension in the air. By the 18th the edge will soften and you can approach the ideas while employing a nurturing attitude and applied intuition. Don't let the fogginess of the 20th send you into despair, remember that what goes up must come down and things will settle again, probably around the 26th when your intuition is inflated. The important transit of summer begins on the 29th. Saturn will retrograde in the creative, intuitive, compassionate sign of Pisces and you can begin to truly assimilate the lessons of your spirituality by asking big questions. Check our retrograde article for more information about this retrograde.

BOOK BONUSES INCLUDE DISCOUNT CODES, EBOOKS, SPECIAL REPORTS, AUDIO FILES AND SPECIAL OFFERS. TO GET ALL THE GOODIES, GO TO
WWW.CHOOSEBIGCHANGE.COM/PAGES/BONUS24

KEY DATES

6/4	**Mercury enters Gemini**
6/6	**New Moon in Gemini,** read moon article
6/10	**Mars enters Taurus**
6/18	**Mercury enters Cancer**
6/18	**Venus enters Cancer**
6/20	**Summer Solstice**
6/21	**Happy Birthday, Cancer**
6/21	**Full Moon in Capricorn,** read moon article
6/26	**Mercury in Cancer trine Saturn in Pisces**
6/29	**Saturn retrograde in Pisces**

♡ Fun, fresh, transformational products + services: https://choosebigchange.com ♡

Copyright © 2023 Tam Veilleux. All rights reserved worldwide.

JUNE PREDICTIONS

MONDAY, JUNE 3 – SUNDAY, JUNE 9

MOONS: TAURUS, GEMINI, CANCER

The first full week of June has you not only enjoying the warmth of late spring but also engaged in visioning yourself using your resources well. Mercury is in its last day of Taurus, encouraging planning and pragmatism with funds. Neptune flavors the day with compassion. It's a lovely start to the week.

On Tuesday, your mind turns curious and your wit amplifies, too, when Mercury enters the sign of Gemini. This planet that rules the lower mind is going to focus on needed changes you might make. Luckily, right behind that, two days later on the June 6th New Moon in Gemini, you can initiate new studies and start gathering information that will move you closer to the goalpost. Catch this month's moon article and suggested affirmations just a few pages from here. Saturday and Sunday there's a couple of cosmic confrontations—there is a sharp clash between Sun and Saturn as well as Venus and Saturn. Tensions arise when curiosity faces spiritual responsibility and profits oppose the same. Will you use your resources well? Will you learn something that can benefit your sacred journey? There's no doubt action will end the crisis. Mind yourself; there is an edge to these aspects that last through Monday.

GIFT & SHADOW THIS WEEK: *We are faced with opposing forces this week—one that wants adventure and experiences and another that feels like "been there, done that" and there's nothing new for me to learn. The first leads us to new experiences that we can share with our fellow humans. It's the story of triumph and exploration. The second one leads us to feel jaded, restless and bored with life and leads us to settle for the status quo. Which will you choose?*

MONDAY, JUNE 10 – SUNDAY, JUNE 16

MOONS: LEO, VIRGO, LIBRA

This week is one for laying low. Monday opens with tenseness and the urge to take action...multiplied! There is stress in the air between no less than five planets. Hear yourself asking: "Will I or won't I?" "Should I or shouldn't I?" Work out the answers by uncovering and understanding your own personal value system and using it as a filter for decision making. Transformation of the group, regenerating ideas about freedom and innovation are all around. The world is changing and you are part of the collective. Choose wisely, little pretzel.

On Wednesday, your lower mind joins the party to analyze and question who is responsible for fulfilling the dream. Who should create the plan? How might it affect your vision? How much compassion is enough or too much? As tension builds, resist the urge to act unless you're certain the timing is right and the outcomes are desirable.

Friday you, or an administrator of sorts, communicates information that might benefit understanding of the ongoings of earlier in the week. Saturday is peaceful and Sunday should you happen upon a bookstore, you might find yourself investing in resources that advance your personal cause, as Neptune is wagging his finger suggesting you buy a book of prayers instead. Choose carefully based on your values.

GIFT & SHADOW THIS WEEK: *What if I told you that prosperity was a natural effect of you aligning with your passion? That is exactly what this week brings us. The potential for monetary gain isn't always linked to what we do. It is more appropriately linked to who we are in our authentic expression. This week, avoid the pressure of doing something just to make money as it is not fulfilling (unless making money is your passion). Know what your passions are—follow them to express yourself in fulfilling and authentic ways. The money or abundance will flow to you effortlessly and naturally.*

☆ Get your book bonus offers: www.choosebigchange.com/pages/bonus24 ☆

Copyright © 2023 Tam Veilleux. All rights reserved worldwide.

MONDAY, JUNE 17 – SUNDAY, JUNE 23

MOONS: SCORPIO, SAGITTARIUS, CAPRICORN

This week brings a softer, kinder feel to the month of June. Monday starts the week with an edge of Sunday's energy. Remind yourself of that energy by rereading last week's prediction.

Tuesday has Mercury, the planet of communication, and Venus, the planet of love and money, both donning the fluffy pink bathrobe of Cancer. Here we have two personal planets wearing the same zodiac, one of high emotion, a love of homelife and nurturing, and a strong intuition. Expect that you will speak with more love and your decision-making will be influenced by how you feel. Partnering will be important and your empathy will be off the charts. Have a handkerchief nearby. On Tuesday these two planets are conjunct, meaning they're sitting on the same cosmic couch. Feeling the feels and analyzing them is part of the day.

Your faith is tested on Thursday and the vision is still a little blurry as you head into the weekend. On Friday your mind is dealing with any lagging frustration and you're ready to move and fight for your own feelings of worthiness. Little Pretzel, it's a moment in time and this too shall pass. Use your energy to take a long walk in the woods or through a meadow. Shake off the despair and see yourself in a new light.

Summer Solstice is this week. Get more in tune with the cycles of nature by experiencing an outdoor Solstice party with friends. Whether you bark at the moon or fall to your knees in prayer, what's important is that you acknowledge the longest day of the year and the coming of the dark. Check out the rituals written by Kara. You're sure to find some solid ideas to use.

The Full Moon in Capricorn is on Friday and it's time to release old ideas about discipline and tradition. Our moon article will guide the way.

GIFT & SHADOW THIS WEEK: *Are you focusing on the light or the dark? This week we learn that what we focus our mind, time, and attention on, holds the power of attraction. Even if we are focused on what we don't want, we are attracting more of that to ourselves. Fear, worry, and anxiety are just as attractive as joy, excitement, and enthusiasm. If we focus on just one little part of the light or one positive thought, it expands and can magnetize more of the light to us. That is a Universal Law!*

ENERGY ALMANAC CHALLENGE: Share photos of your Summer Solstice Celebration. We'd love to see how you do your rituals. Tag us using @TheEnergyAlmanac so we can say a prayer for you.

Copyright © 2023 Tam Veilleux. All rights reserved worldwide.

MONDAY, JUNE 24 – SUNDAY, JUNE 30

MOONS: AQUARIUS, PISCES, ARIES

The last week of June starts gently under the rebel-with-a-cause Aquarian moon. Enjoy leaning into your intuition on both Monday and Tuesday. On Wednesday, Mercury in Cancer has you feeling into ideas concerning your deservingness. You may have sudden inspirations about why you feel the way you do and can put plans into place that will benefit you. Thursday through Sunday, Venus in Cancer will skip across the cosmos with Mars. They form a sextile. They are both stimulated and happy to cooperate. Mars is currently engaged with your personal resources while Venus is deeply planted in the empathetic sign of Cancer. Together these two encourage new ways to serve your own well-being. Honor yourself with kind thoughts, feed yourself with the best foods, nurture your own self-worth over the next few days and expect some personal growth.

On Sunday you could think quite differently. Outside of the box ideas about your budget will come out of nowhere. Enjoy the cosmic ride.

GIFT & SHADOW THIS WEEK: *This week concerns our ability to know what to focus our time and attention on. In the shadow this can feel like ADD—when we have a feeling of so much to do that we end up zipping from one thing to another without ever finishing. Sometimes it is stillness that is called for. A pause before taking action to gain clarity over what the step is. This week, learn that relaxation is a stress reliever and taking on too much or feeling pushed to do it all, creates stress.*

- FEELING STUCK AND LOSING SLEEP OVER PAST MISTAKES?
- STILL STRUGGLING TO FEEL SUCCESSFUL OR BELIEVE IN YOURSELF?

HELP YOURSELF TO CLARITY AND CONFIDENCE WITH EFT TAPPING. IN ONLY 21 DAYS YOU CAN ELIMINATE YEARS OF HABITUAL NEGATIVE THOUGHT PATTERNS AND CREATE THE BIG SHIFT YOU CRAVE.

HTTPS://CHOOSEBIGCHANGE.COM/PRODUCTS/21-DAY-EMOTIONAL-DETOX

Copyright © 2023 Tam Veilleux. All rights reserved worldwide.

JUNE 6, 8:38 AM EDT
NEW MOON AT 16° GEMINI

HAVE MORE FUN

Gemini is extroverted and always looks for excitement. This trait pairs well with the unlimited potential of a new moon. Let the fun-loving energy seep into all areas of your life, especially where things are being taken too seriously.

The Gemini twins are also hanging out with Mercury, Venus, and Jupiter right now. Creativity is coming out in all forms, and inspiration is coming from everywhere. We're rediscovering the autonomy we have over ourselves and our lives. Don't be surprised if fresh revelations come through on lifestyle choices.

Success rates are running high right now—good news for us moon manifestors! The energies now are supporting ethical influence, guiding us to take action and make connections we might not realize are options.

Look to your favorite kinds of media for fresh inspiration. Explore new art, music, and literature for fun, interesting insights into spirituality. Those big dream seeds have grown into little saplings, so keep it up! Gemini is *obsessed* with progress and is more than motivated to maintain momentum.

AFFIRMATION: ***"Life is full of excitement and enjoyment! Manifesting is fun and easy."***

MONTHLY MOONWORK:

- Schedule a grown-up playdate with people who make you laugh.
- See at least one new piece of art, go to at least one new place, and hear at least one new song.
- Look for boring pockets in your mundane life and inject them with fun.

♡ Fun, fresh, transformational products + services: https://choosebigchange.com ♡

Copyright © 2023 Tam Veilleux. All rights reserved worldwide.

JUNE 21, 9:08 PM EDT

FULL MOON 1° CAPRICORN

RESPECTFUL DREAM CHASING

Capricorn is the most driven and ambitious sign in astrology. It loves being busy, and Mercury sextile Mars is adding fuel to this fire. But Full Moons don't feel like busy times for most people. Really tune in to see how *your* body and soul are responding to the energy.

Tackling an oversized to-do list may feel *amazing* right now. This energy is too good to use on the mundane lists, though. Use this energy to tackle your *big dream* to-do list. You'll likely find you suddenly have the courage you lacked before.

It's important now to keep grounded on Earth, as some very practical advice is making its way to us. We're being guided to handle our relationships maturely.

Translation: have respectful grown-up conversations, not arguments. And if you find that someone else isn't feeling this Venus-in-Capricorn approach, at least you can say you tried. Then you can adjust your expectations and let go of what's not serving the relationship.

AFFIRMATION: ***"My relationships are respectful. I take steps toward my dreams every single day. I love overcoming challenges!"***

MONTHLY MOONWORK:

- Treat others with respect, the way you would like to be treated.
- Embrace courage and have those hard conversations.
- Heed any advice given to you that resonates with your soul.

Copyright © 2023 Tam Veilleux. All rights reserved worldwide.

Numerology

After taking a little pause in May to evaluate your life and projects, June arrives with the balanced and calm energy of the 6 and blends with the strong manifesting energy of the 8 year to create a very high energy of the 5 (6 + 8 = 14, 1 + 4 = 5). The 5 energy is very active and does not want to sit still or become stagnant. This is a month for you to get things done. Take action. Almost, as if in fear of becoming stagnant, the 5 energy wants change and variety. This is the time to make any change that is needed after your evaluations last month. Shift your direction if needed and when you're sure you're on the right path—buckle up and get busy.

Aromatherapy & Gemstones

AROMAS: CITRONELLA & CEDARWOOD Happy thoughts are joyful experiences in our mind that shape how we view ourselves and the world around us. June's aromas, Citronella & Cedarwood are uplifting and stress-reducing fragrances. This combination is your reminder to practice happy thinking every day.

The combination of Citronella & Cedarwood aromas are easily recognized for the sweet, woodsy, and citrusy fragrance. They are typically associated with candles lit during summer nights, hiking, camping, or the great outdoors and used to keep mosquitoes at bay.

What you are thinking, you are manifesting and what you focus on, you create more of. Citronella & Cedarwood are naturally uplifting and cheerful. It is your ideal companion this month as you release tensions, simplify, and turn the volume up on your happy thoughts. Be delighted as more and more joy makes its way towards you.

GEMSTONE: CARNELIAN Carnelian gemstones are deeply passionate stones that encourage you to stay in your power. This stone is highly stimulating. It will bring you the courage you need to transform.

Let Carnelian crystals do the job of clearing away any negative energies that may surround you. Let its protective forces bring you grounded confidence and courage to be here in the present moment. The very moment you feel supported by the ground beneath your feet is the very moment you will be ready to take a leap forward.

You are strong. You are courageous. You are ready to transform.

ACCESS THE ENERGIES:

- Diffuse a blend of 3-4 drops of Citronella & Cedarwood essential oils at dusk each day.
- Keep a Carnelian gemstone in your pocket or wear a piece of jewelry. Carry its passionate and courageous energy with you throughout your day.

♡ Fun, fresh, transformational products + services: https://choosebigchange.com ♡

Copyright © 2023 Tam Veilleux. All rights reserved worldwide.

The Tarot card associated with Gemini is **The Lovers**. The Lovers is a card that represents choices, partnerships, and relationships of any kind. It is a card of harmony, connection, and balance. It encourages us to explore our desires, to make choices based on our values, and to connect with others in meaningful ways. The Lovers can also suggest a need for communication, understanding, and cooperation.

In Gemini season, you are supported to make choices that align with your values and to cultivate healthy relationships based on mutual respect and understanding.

THE LOVERS AFFIRMATION ***"I am balanced and in harmony with myself and my surroundings and collaborate with ease in all relationships."***

Merry Meet! Our days are growing, as our nights give way. Litha, the Solstice, is the magic of light and dark sharing time. This creates kairos, the perfect moment, the creation, the atmosphere for movement, action, magic. Our Sun sends hints of encouragement, hope and enlightenment. The night shows us shadows of dreams of the future, of the possibilities that abound. This is a time of abundance, fullness, and life. Use this day to be with nature, perhaps in your own garden or next to water on a sandy beach. Maybe you'll choose a forest park where you have camped the night before or a private spot along a creek. You shall draw in the elements, earth, water, air and fire.

LITHA DAY ELEMENT RITUAL

Arise at the Blue Hour, the moments of time before the Sun breaks the horizon and the sky glows blue with anticipation. Find your place to be in the sunrise, perhaps your Cynefin.

EARTH Collect your elements to make a Solstice offering, which is a mandala, left for others to enjoy as they happen upon your magic. Harmlessly gather natural elements to form your mandala. Leaves, twigs, flowers, rocks all do well. Shape them into a mandala that whispers to your heart. Leave an offering from you. Let the sunrise shine upon your face. This is earth element.

WATER As the Sun climbs in the sky, in a space where the sunbeams will alight, place a vessel. For you shall make Sun tea. Fill your vessel with warm water. Place your tea into the vessel. Choose tea that you love, black, white, green or herb, bags, or loose. Stir clockwise, 3 times. Let the tea steep as the Sun moves across the sky. This is water element.

AIR Stand in stillness, as the golden hour arrives. Face the Sun as it meets the horizon. Take a deep breath. With your dominant hand, draw a Caim around you, an invisible circle of protection, draw 3 circles. No matter the darkness, you are safe. This is air element.

FIRE As the last of the light fades from the golden sky, light your fire. Once the flames are amber at the peak and clear blue within, add herbs:

Pine for protection
Lavender for luck
Sage for wisdom
Salt for protection

Watch the fire burn down as the stars appear. In the light of the new day, come back to your fire and gather ashes to keep the magic with you through to the next Litha. This is fire element. Merry Part!

Copyright © 2023 Tam Veilleux. All rights reserved worldwide.

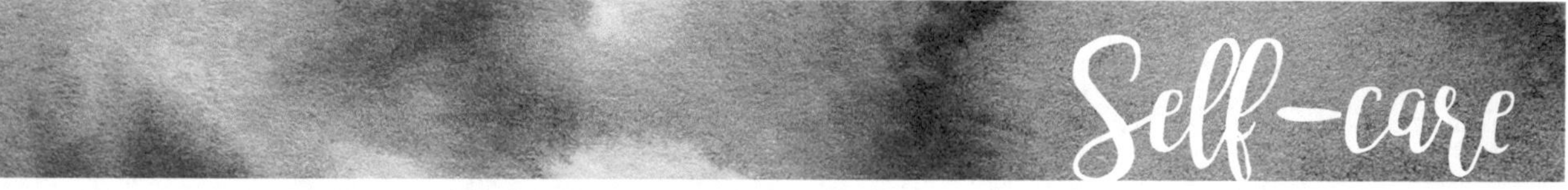

Pitta season is here! Pitta is a combination of both fire and water so when you combine them it gets steamy. This is a time when the weather is getting hotter and more humid. As the environment changes, so do your body and mind. When you have a pitta imbalance in your system, it can show up as inflammation, acne or blemishes, diarrhea, headaches, interrupted sleep, heartburn and indigestion. Your mind can become more easily frustrated, irritable, judgmental, and you are more prone to burnout.

In order to stay in balance over the next few months, it is important to incorporate cooling foods and activities in your daily routine. It is best to avoid spicy, fried foods, caffeine, and alcohol. Favor foods like smoothies, juices, fruits, seeds, nuts, and salads. Avoid hot yoga classes and high-intensity exercise routines. Favor activities like swimming, restorative yoga, and going for a walk in nature around dusk or dawn. Meditation also has a calming and cooling effect on the mind.

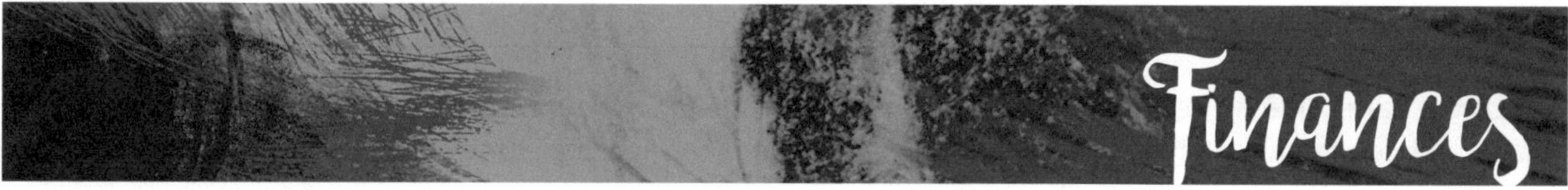

Do you ever wonder why the rich get richer and the poor get? Oh, I know you know the answer to that. It's a very old cliché that I wish was not true, but it is. There's a reason for this though and it boils down to a few things, one of which is EDUCATION. And if you are one of the few who gained that education growing up, YAY for you! It's a really great thing when it does happen.

For the rest of us though, there is some catching up to do. I'm not sure what you were taught in school, but I know for me, other than that accounting class I took, I didn't learn anything about the real business of money. I'm learning now though and I want to teach you how money works too.

This is a great month to look at your budget and see if it is working for you. If not, what thoughts are dominant, what is your intuition nudging you towards? Are you being real with your money or are you dreaming up and scheming things that aren't going to happen?

Go to the Energy Almanac Bonus Page (www.choosebigchange.com/pages/bonus24) to get your free You're The One Journal to learn more about your budget, let's do this!

♡ Fun, fresh, transformational products + services: https://choosebigchange.com ♡

Copyright © 2023 Tam Veilleux. All rights reserved worldwide.

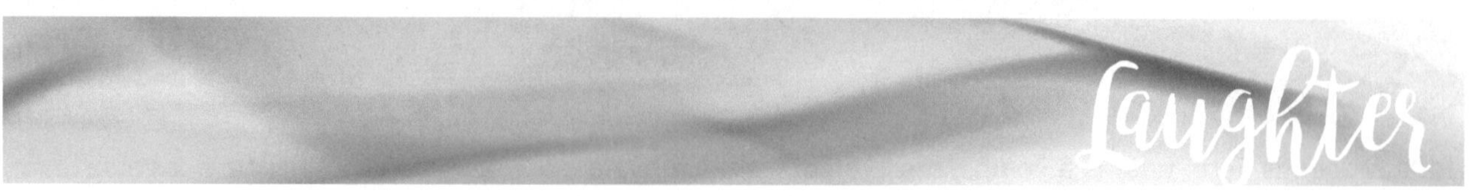

Because this is the month where students are getting out of school, this is the perfect time to bring other people in on the laughter exercises with you.

"Often what makes us laugh is when our brain is expecting one thing and then, in the space of a few words, that expectation is turned on its head," says Scott Weems, a research scientist at the University of Maryland College Park, and the author of *Ha!: The Science of When We Laugh and Why*.

This is why Mad Libs, "the world's greatest word game," has been so successful since its first publication in 1958. The game itself consists of one player prompting others for a list of words to substitute for blanks in a story before reading aloud. This month, I want you to create your own Mad Libs Laughter. Find a story that everyone in your family or social circle knows and then randomly replace some of the adjectives, adverbs, nouns, and verbs with other words. I guarantee that before the new story is written, you will already be laughing together.

Laughter Yoga promotes a strong union between those who laugh together resulting in family like bonds, providing social interactions and networking—all are essential to creating a feeling of happiness.

Notes

Get your book bonus offers: www.choosebigchange.com/pages/bonus24

Copyright © 2023 Tam Veilleux. All rights reserved worldwide.

RECONSIDERING LOVE

JULY 1 – 7

DO liberate yourself from a lack mindset.
DO NOT be stubborn.

JULY 8 – 14

DO watch for changes in the economy.
DO NOT push to make something happen.

JULY 15 – 21

DO mind the details.
DO NOT be overly nit picky.

JULY 22 – 28

DO temper your words and actions.
DO NOT be overly critical of yourself.

IT IS SAFE FOR ME TO AMPLIFY AND EMPLOY SPIRITUAL PRACTICES.

JULY 5, 6:57 PM EDT

NEW MOON AT 14° CANCER
KEEP MANIFESTING

JULY 21, 6:17 AM EDT

FULL MOON AT 29° CAPRICORN
SHAKE IT OFF

♡ Love the Energy Almanac? Tag us on social media: @TheEnergyAlmanac ♡
Copyright © 2023 Tam Veilleux. All rights reserved worldwide.

July

The bright, warm light of July offers plenty of time for basking, but be sure you carry your journal when you're at the beach. With two outer planets in retrograde, there is some inner work going on. On the second of the month, Neptune, the planet of spirituality, currently in the sign of Pisces, wants you to internalize your spiritual practice and look again at your dreams of the future while Saturn retrograde in Pisces asks you to question your integrity, timing, and self-authority toward your faith. Honestly, if you aren't questioning your relationship to Source at this time, it would be a real surprise! Alongside these retrogrades are some delightful transits to play with. Mid-month, watch the 14th through the 16th when Mars and Uranus, both in Taurus, have you itching to take action toward adjusting your resources. Maybe you'll rewrite the budget, acquire some new goods, or finally take a hard look at your own self-worth. While the Sun is in Cancer you may feel the need to hang with the family and soak up the rays as you pour the family some lemonade and rub sunblock on them, all the while cooking up new ways to nurture their faith. There's playful energy tickling your unconscious when the Sun enters Leo. The days for thinking up new ways to enjoy yourself happen between the 24th and 29th. Then let the month fade and the Sun set slowly in July as you speak prayers for humanitarian shifts that are underway. The Neptune-Pluto transit occurring during the last four days of the month will tug your heart in this manner.

BOOK BONUSES INCLUDE DISCOUNT CODES, EBOOKS, SPECIAL REPORTS, AUDIO FILES AND SPECIAL OFFERS. TO GET ALL THE GOODIES, GO TO
WWW.CHOOSEBIGCHANGE.COM/PAGES/BONUS24

KEY DATES

Saturn retrograde all month

7/2	**Neptune retrogrades in Pisces**
7/3	**Mercury enters Leo**
7/5	**New Moon in Cancer,** read moon article
7/12	**Venus enters Leo**
7/21	**Mars enters Gemini**
7/21	**Full Moon in Capricorn,** read moon article
7/23	**Happy Birthday, Leo**
7/26	**Mercury enters Virgo**
7/28-31	**Neptune sextile Pluto**

Copyright © 2023 Tam Veilleux. All rights reserved worldwide.

JULY PREDICTIONS

MONDAY, JULY 1 – SUNDAY, JULY 7

MOONS: TAURUS, GEMINI, CANCER, LEO

The first of July finds you emotional about your visions but the planets are kind. Saturn is playing nicely with Venus and Neptune, suggesting you take responsibility for your connection to Source—bring order to how you connect and honor it. It's an opportunity ripe with compassion for yourself. Tap in, tune in and listen to the inner guidance that will surely come on Wednesday and Thursday. Don't be stubborn. Mercury is in Leo now and creative expression is charged with drama about humanity's impending transformation. Rather than let the drama rise, seek ways to share what you know without all the song and dance. The moon in Cancer is a chance to nurture your intuition and mother yourself. Read our moon article for more information about this lunation happening on Friday. Also present starting Thursday and ending Saturday is Mars sextile Saturn, where your urge to act for the benefit of your financial condition is being activated and supported by a sense of personal responsibility.

GIFT & SHADOW THIS WEEK: *Liberation from lack. Doesn't that sound wonderful? This week brings us the opportunity to transform challenges into opportunities to shift to greater abundance. It turns out that this is all about re-calibrating ourselves to align with abundance as it is a birthright rather than something we must struggle to achieve. We also have to face whether or not we are "enough" or have enough and what do we do when we don't feel enough? Weight issues, hoarding, and over-shopping are all symptoms of our trying to fill the void of "not enough." Trusting in a higher power and having faith in our deservingness serve to elevate us out of lack and into abundance.*

MONDAY, JULY 8 – SUNDAY, JULY 14

MOONS: LEO, VIRGO, LIBRA

Week 2 starts with your mind conjuring up bold ways of finding answers or perhaps leading a social gathering with your charm. Manage your emotions as new ideas about your own self-worth fill you. Wednesday and Thursday could find you highly intuitive and equally emotional. The real transit to watch is when the warrior planet Mars shares cosmic space with the rebel-with-a-cause planet Uranus who is trying to create change. Both planets are in the denim overalls of Taurus which deals with our pragmatic application of resources. This fascinating aspect, which will last from Sunday to Tuesday, could create the urge to revamp your budget, revisit your investment portfolio, or finally address any feelings of unworthiness. On a much grander scale, watch for some rearrangement of the global economy to come out of nowhere.

GIFT & SHADOW THIS WEEK: *Force and flow are the energies in the gift and shadow this week. Force becomes a shadow when we are inspired to do something and then, rather than waiting for Divine timing, we push or try to make something happen. Flow is the opposite. Flow is established when we are divinely inspired to do something and then we wait and watch for what is opening up in front of us, prompting us to make our move. We also notice when the flow seems to be ebbing and take that as a sign to rest, wait, or be patient until the flow resumes again. Don't let the pressure cause you to make things happen.*

✯ Get your book bonus offers: www.choosebigchange.com/pages/bonus24 ✯

Copyright © 2023 Tam Veilleux. All rights reserved worldwide.

MONDAY, JULY 15 – SUNDAY, JULY 21	**MOONS**: SCORPIO, SAGITTARIUS, CAPRICORN

As Monday opens, you're still handling the Mars-Uranus conjunction in the sign of Taurus. Please reread last week's prediction for possibilities as those energies are present through Tuesday. Wednesday until Friday find yourself tuned in energetically and intuitively to incoming ideas. Some new experiments may be at hand and you're likely to take intuitively guided actions such as journaling outcomes, automatic writing, or chanting your way through the emotion of it all. "How can I break free from self-perceived limitations?" is one good question you can work with under this transit.

On Saturday the 20th, resources and a sense of deep faith sprinkled with deep compassion meld nicely and it's a good day for making a vision board, writing a story about your abundant future or taking a class about spiritual investment practices. Sunday is singing an entirely different song—the last day of this week is a Full Moon in Capricorn, and finds Mars entering Gemini, the sign of the student. The Sun, Neptune, Mercury, Uranus, Venus, Jupiter, Mars, and Pluto are all having a cosmic gathering. Some are playing nicely (Sun trine Neptune has you deeply intuitive and highly emotional) and some planets are squaring off (Mercury and Venus). For a detailed view of this Full Moon, do read the article further on in this month's writing because really, it's a cosmic party and you want to be prepared.

GIFT & SHADOW THIS WEEK: *Mind the details this week, but don't lose sight of the forest either. We have to avoid being overly nitpicky with the details, however. Part of the energy this week is about being prepared but not being so worried about all the details that we trigger fear and worry and even overwhelm. Instead, trust that we will have everything we need in the right moment. Don't get trapped this week by feeling like we need to do more and more in order to be ready. Relax.*

ENERGY ALMANAC CHALLENGE: How did the Mars-Uranus conjunction affect your world? Share your thoughts via a post on FB or IG. Tag us with @theenergyalmanac so we can share the love.

♡ Fun, fresh, transformational products + services: https://choosebigchange.com ♡

Copyright © 2023 Tam Veilleux. All rights reserved worldwide.

MONDAY, JULY 22 – SUNDAY, JULY 28

MOONS: AQUARIUS, PISCES, ARIES, TAURUS

The final days of July are upon us and Monday has many of the luminaries still playing ring around the rosy. It's a day where you feel like talking about your dreams of the future and sharing your ideas about faith, but have tissues close by as you're likely to trigger some feelings. Pluto wants your contribution to the good of the whole and you surely feel the desire to nurture others, but there's a home life to tend to…now what? You'll likely need to compromise to find the right balance. Your communication about how to address change may be a little too playful to be taken seriously and at the same time, you feel an abundance of passion about your many inclinations. It's a wildly spicy soup on Monday and Tuesday. It's best to temper your tongue and feet. Don't speak too quickly or move on your ideas too soon. Slow and steady wins the race, Little Pretzel.

Mercury is changing costumes again this month, this time donning the lab coat of the analytical Virgo. You may notice a more judgmental you or a heart for service. Your mind may move quite quickly—do apply its energy appropriately.

One of the final transits of July showcases you as the star athlete hungry to learn more, share more, and be seen. Many social events aside, we're pretty sure you'll be thinking up new ways to enjoy yourself but watch that your passion isn't mistaken for aggression as you share what you know. And always remember to walk your talk!

GIFT & SHADOW THIS WEEK: *This week carries on a bit of last week's gift and shadow except we are dealing with issues around perfection. We must learn to trust that we are perfect exactly as we are right now. To become overly critical of ourself or others leads to becoming judgmental and no one has time for that! So see that everything is working out in our favor, and even if we don't feel like it's perfect, it really is!*

FUN, FRESH, TRANSFORMATIONAL COMPANION PRODUCTS TO HELP MAKE 2024 AMAZING ARE AVAILABLE AT:

WWW.CHOOSEBIGCHANGE.COM

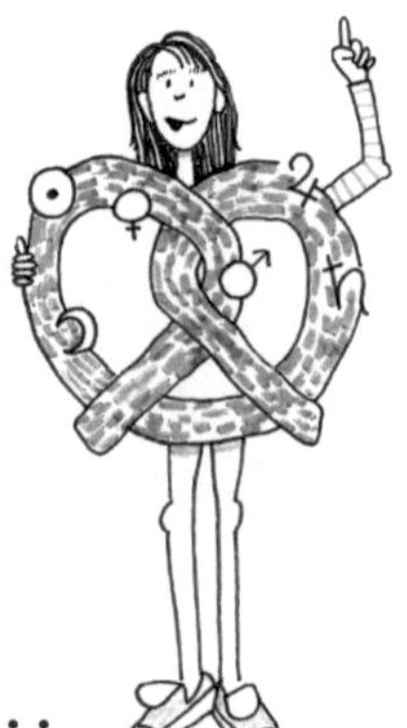

Copyright © 2023 Tam Veilleux. All rights reserved worldwide.

JULY 5, 6:57 PM EDT
NEW MOON AT 14° CANCER

KEEP MANIFESTING

Emotions run intensely deep with Cancer. We're yearning for more intimacy and emotional stability within our relationships now. Speak from the heart, loudly and clearly, so there's no confusion on needs, intentions, and expectations.

The more mindful we are about our emotions, the easier it will be to stay the course. Use this month's new moon energy to set intentions around emotional stability through self-reflection.

Mars and Saturn are conspiring to enhance our endurance today. We may not be making long strides forward while Saturn travels backward. But we have more than enough stamina and patience than ever.

Just in time too, because the manifesting high brought on by the spring super-moon cycle has dwindled. We need perseverance to see our manifestations fully realized.

Focus is imperative now. Those big dream saplings are still growing! Don't forget to keep nurturing them, even if it feels like a grind. All our heavy lifting is paying off quickly.

AFFIRMATION: *"My hard work always pays off in the most magical way!"*

MONTHLY MOONWORK:

- Vocalize your relationship needs and expectations to boost intimacy and emotional fulfillment.
- Keep going! Whatever you've been doing to nurture your big dream seeds, keep doing it.
- Make a list of all things you've already accomplished and/or manifested this year so far to remind you how well you're doing.

♡ Fun, fresh, transformational products + services: https://choosebigchange.com ♡

Copyright © 2023 Tam Veilleux. All rights reserved worldwide.

JULY 21, 6:17 AM EDT FULL MOON AT 29° CAPRICORN	SHAKE IT OFF

Capricorn is the most driven and ambitious sign in astrology. It loves being busy, but Full Moons don't feel like busy times for most people. Shake out those jitters so they don't disrupt your flow of abundance.

The Cosmos are *insisting* we come out of the spiritual closet now. It's time to show the world our spiritual specialties. No more hiding our love of spirituality and all that comes with it (astrology, tarot, crystals, essential oils, etc.!). It's only hindering our expansion and manifestations.

Capricorn is highly motivated and is prone to impatience if it feels progress isn't being made. While Mercury and Uranus square off, it may feel even more difficult to cultivate staying power. We want new experiences and we want them now.

We're feeling more willful and determined than ever before. Whatever is standing in our way *must* go. But all good things come to those who wait, and to those who intentionally let go of what no longer serves them.

AFFIRMATION: *"It's safe to authentically express my spiritual self."*

MONTHLY MOONWORK:

- Dance, party, and make love! Venus sextile Jupiter is begging you for some romantic fun.
- Practice patience, because it's the most important manifesting skill you can cultivate.
- Shake off whatever doesn't serve your manifestations. Capricorn doesn't have time to entertain what's not in alignment.

☆ Get your book bonus offers: www.choosebigchange.com/pages/bonus24 ☆

Copyright © 2023 Tam Veilleux. All rights reserved worldwide.

Numerology

You may be ready to catch your breath after last month, and July is a good time and energy for that. July has the introspective energy of the 7 and blends with the manifesting 8 year to create a balanced and harmonious 6 energy (7 + 8 = 15, 1 + 5 = 6). The 6 energy loves peace and calm and it's all about family, home, relationships, and communication. This is a great time to make sure you communicate with and include your family and close friends, partners, or team in on your projects and goals. You may have been so focused that you've just been going at it alone. Including your community and even having their perspective on things, can bring a few things to light that you may have overlooked. Otherwise, just having their support and cheering you on can give you more confidence and your projects extra strength.

Aromatherapy & Gemstones

AROMAS: SWEET LEMON & MINT This month's aromas are Sweet Lemon & Mint. It is a sweet, zesty, cheerful fragrance with invigorating properties that will give you an uplifting, positive boost.

Summer gives us good grounds to rest and relax; the heat makes us want to move slower. It is important, however, to notice the habits that you adopt or repeat in your life. Don't let this summertime slow-down manifest itself into lethargic energy.

Every moment is a chance to create a new habit that serves you. Sweet Lemon & Mint are bright and positive aromas that will give you the boost of playful energy and clarity you need to get in the groove and out of the rut this month.

GEMSTONE: CITRINE It's July and we are surrounded by lemonade, honey and all things bright and sunny. But even in the sunny summer months, it is possible to feel like you are in the dark and you may need help finding your inner light and enough-ness again.

This month, if and when you need an extra boost of positivity, let Citrine Crystals be the sunshine to your darkness, the happiness to your melancholy. Citrine Crystals want you to feel joy in every way possible. They are your powerfully positive cheerleader who is here to remind you that: You are enough. You have enough. You do enough.

ACCESS THE ENERGIES:

- Create a stovetop potpourri using lemon slices & mint or diffuse a blend of 3-4 drops of Lemon & Mint essential oils.
- Place your Citrine crystal in your office to attract positive energy throughout your day.

Copyright © 2023 Tam Veilleux. All rights reserved worldwide.

The Tarot card associated with Cancer is **The Chariot**. The Chariot is a card that represents victory, control, and determination. It is a card of motivation, ambition, and willpower. It encourages us to take action by using heart and head, to stay focused on our goals, and to overcome obstacles with confidence and courage. The Chariot can also suggest a need for balance, self-discipline, and assertiveness.

In Cancer season, you may, once again, feel a need to assert yourself, to take charge of your life, and to move forward with determination and purpose. This is also a season that supports change and travel.

THE CHARIOT AFFIRMATION *"I am moving towards my desires and making necessary changes that are aligned with my heart and soul."*

Merry Meet!
Ahh, we are now basking in the bright and warm days of summer. At this yearly mid-point we are captivated by our two sides. Our Sun side feels the glowing fullness around us. The Earth is lush and plentiful and we join in. Our days are creative and our sultry nights are brimming with secrets. Our moon side wonders if we can see our path. In the darkness, we are seeking our truth and where that will lead our hearts and actions. Now, do not think just one of your sides has the power to create the energy we need. One side is not whole without the other. You must be intentional in joining your sides, to create your Querencia, your soul place where you find your strength, and your true authentic self.

QUERENCIA RITUAL

Choose your spell jar and cleanse with 3 soft breaths.

Cast together:

- Rice for abundance
- Salt for strength of purpose
- Cloves to bring love
- Sage for positive vibes and actions
- Lavender for peace of mind
- Rosemary for clarity of mind
- Marjoram to bring insight

Place a special talisman to focus the intentions specifically on you. Seal your jar with white wax. Hold your jar to your heart often to find your Querencia. Merry part!

✯ Get your book bonus offers: www.choosebigchange.com/pages/bonus24 ✯
Copyright © 2023 Tam Veilleux. All rights reserved worldwide.

You are a multi-dimensional being! Oftentimes we are highly connected to our mind, but disconnected from our body and spirit. It is important to have a healthy, intimate relationship with each aspect of your being, and they all need different types of self-care. This month you may be feeling more inspired to connect with your spirit and your relationship to Source. This makes it a great time to focus on your crown chakra. Find the link for self-care on the bonus page for a simple guided relaxation that will help you get in touch with your spirit and balance your crown chakra.

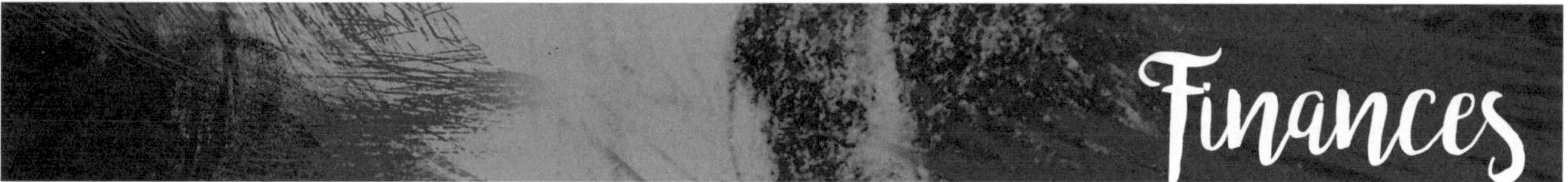

Self-Worth and Faith are the topics this month and they do play into your money patterning. I'm going to ask you a few more questions to prompt how you feel about money. Some of these are similar, but each time they are asked, it flushes out another layer of truth.

Take a breath all the way into your abdomen. Hold for a few seconds. Then release tension, anxiety, and thoughts that do not serve you. Repeat a few times and answer the following questions:

1. Do I feel worthy of money flow coming into my life?
2. Do I have faith that no matter what happens money wise, I will be ok?
3. What did my parents teach me about money?
4. What is my predominant mood when I think about money?
5. Am I overspending? If so, where?
6. Am I leaking money? Meaning, do I know where every penny is going?
7. Do I tithe? If yes, is it with money or time or both?

That will keep you busy writing in your You're The One Journal. Take time with this, it is important to figure these things out so that you can Know Yourself and understand your patterns.

The height of summer is upon us and that means spending more time outdoors. This is the perfect opportunity to practice **Laughter Ball**.

You can do this activity by yourself, with a partner, or even in a group. Take an invisible (or soft) ball and begin playing catch with it. As you throw the ball to one another—you laugh. Whoever is holding the ball should be laughing. You can also dribble the ball and laugh each time it hits the floor.

Laughing for up to 10 to 15 minutes a day can burn an extra 50 calories. And, guess what? One piece of chocolate has about 50 calories; at the rate of 50 calories per hour, losing one pound would require about 12 hours of concentrated laughter!

How long can you play Laughter Ball for? The longer you play, the more chocolate you can eat!

♡ Fun, fresh, transformational products + services: https://choosebigchange.com ♡

Copyright © 2023 Tam Veilleux. All rights reserved worldwide.

Copyright © 2023 Tam Veilleux. All rights reserved worldwide.

August

SYNTHESIZING LOVE AND CHANGE

JULY 29 – AUGUST 4

DO address old stories and beliefs.
DO NOT overindulge in spending.

AUGUST 5 – 11

DO expect a slower pace.
DO NOT avoid collaboration.

AUGUST 12 – 18

DO be open-minded this week.
DO NOT shut down to new possibilities.

AUGUST 19 – 25

DO enter into commitments carefully.
DO NOT avoid your spiritual practices.

IT IS SAFE FOR ME TO ASSIMILATE OLD INFORMATION AND LEARN TO LOVE CHANGE.

AUGUST 4, 7:13 AM EDT

NEW MOON AT 12° LEO

CALL FOR BACKUP

AUGUST 19, 2:26 PM EDT

FULL MOON AT 27° AQUARIUS

RESPONSIBLY FREE

♡ Love the Energy Almanac? Tag us on social media: @TheEnergyAlmanac ♡

Copyright © 2023 Tam Veilleux. All rights reserved worldwide.

August opens with a slow roll. Three planets are retrograde and Mercury will join them for a truly introspective month covering many life areas, making it the perfect time for relaxing into self-care and digging into full comprehension of old information. As a reminder, Neptune, Pluto, and Saturn are all retrograde. This covers areas including spirituality and faith, restructuring of the group and of freedom in the future. A good question to keep asking is, "What am I learning right now that can benefit myself and others?" When Mercury joins the retro-party in his fancy Virgo lab coat, you can enjoy time bringing order to your environment. Feel free to redo your rooms, your pantry, and evaluate your health. The second part of Mercury retrograde is in Leo starting on the 16th. Here's your opportunity to address creative expression and how well you play. How about reimagining how you play?! *(**Note from Author, less work and more play makes us all happier and brings us closer to God!)* August isn't all journaling, by the way. Look for some big energy to play out in the middle of the month when we get to experience a T-Square and a Grand Trine. These cosmic events have real teeth and will move the world toward optimism and hope, and a redirecting of what we currently believe. The T-Square on August 17th is the day to lean into your faith, and ten days later you can use your tactical skills for addressing the future. Hang in there as the vision is cloudy for a few days. Let the fog settle as you slide into September.

BOOK BONUSES INCLUDE DISCOUNT CODES, EBOOKS, SPECIAL REPORTS, AUDIO FILES AND SPECIAL OFFERS. TO GET ALL THE GOODIES, GO TO
WWW.CHOOSEBIGCHANGE.COM/PAGES/BONUS24

KEY DATES

Saturn, Neptune, Pluto retrograde

8/1-31	**Neptune in Pisces sextile Pluto in Aquarius all month**—love and change
8/4	**New Moon in Leo,** read moon article
8/5-15	**Mercury retrograde in Virgo**
8/6	**Venus enters Virgo**
8/16-27	**Mercury retrograde in Leo**
8/17	**T-Square, Jupiter and Mars in Gemini squaring Saturn in Pisces and Venus in Virgo**
8/19	**Full Moon in Aquarius,** read moon article
8/23	**Happy Birthday, Virgo**
8/27	**Grand Trine with Venus, Pluto, Uranus**
8/28	**Mercury stations direct in Leo**
8/30	**Venus enters Libra**

Copyright © 2023 Tam Veilleux. All rights reserved worldwide.

AUGUST PREDICTIONS

MONDAY, JULY 29 – SUNDAY, AUGUST 4

MOONS: GEMINI, CANCER, LIBRA

Monday through Wednesday wraps up July with you sharing the drama of the previous weekend. Don't let those stories stall you, and don't be overly zealous in how you share. Do save the drama for your Mama. August 1st begins an entire month of Neptune tickling Pluto. Neptune is influencing love, spirituality, and compassion, and Pluto is influencing freedom, groups of people, and innovation. Together, these two luminaries are going to play in your psyche working toward creating a transcendent transformation. All month long, allow your dreams to show you how to best contribute to the changes needed on the planet. Ask yourself: "How can love play a bigger part in decision making?" In other news this week, on Thursday your flirty nature and passion for playfulness could be found bothersome to ideas about the changing economy. You want to dance, but there's no money for a new dress. Think entertainment on a shoestring. The need to be practical could be at hand, so decide carefully. We know it's a Friday night—checkers anyone? Speaking of money, check into our articles on money. There's plenty to learn about mindset, self-worth, and stacking bills.

By the way, Mercury is in the shade period and next week it goes full on retrograde in the analytical sign of Virgo. Wrap things up this week and lay low next.

Sunday is the New Moon in the playful sign of Leo. Be sure to glance the article further along in this month's reading to understand the drama this one may bring.

GIFT & SHADOW THIS WEEK: *What old beliefs, patterns, and experiences are you clinging to? This week we get the opportunity to address the stories we tell ourselves about any number of things. Addressing them means rewriting them! We tend to tell the stories of our experiences in the same way over and over again. It's time to elevate and tell the story of how you overcame struggle and strife and trauma. It's not what happened so much as it is what did you learn from the experience and how did the experience serve to help you evolve your consciousness?*

MONDAY, AUGUST 5 – SUNDAY, AUGUST 11

MOONS: LEO, VIRGO, LIBRA, SCORPIO

This week, Mercury goes retrograde in Virgo. Your opportunity for bringing order to everything is here. August is the month to clean closets, drawers, mindset issues, and any environmental distraction. Always of service, Virgo is the great doer. Victim to their own overdoing, this is a perfect time to think of your own oversharing of time and effort. Rework your schedule and assimilate old information about your behaviors. This transit lasts until the 15th when Mercury will enter Leo. We'll talk about that next week.

On Tuesday the planet of love and money, Venus, will enter Virgo for most of the rest of the month giving the month of August a real feel of pragmatic pleasure. Notice you feel more careful and cautious inside of love and finances. A seriousness spikes partnerships. Maybe the two of you will join forces for some retrograde work by diving into journal sessions, long walks where you suss out answers for the grand scheme. Because, Little Pretzel, August is about slowing down. Multiple planets are retrograde and you shouldn't expect momentum. Moreover, you should plan down time and deep contemplation on a hammock. These are all perfect ideas for a Venus in Virgo transit.

GIFT & SHADOW THIS WEEK: *Collaboration, cooperation, and co-creation are the gifts this week brings when we stop struggling to be seen and heard as "the leader." But the opposite may also be true. We may have dissolved so much into the group that we have lost our own individuality. This week, find the balance between teamwork and "me" work. As we evolve more and more consciousness, you will naturally find that middle ground where you are valued as much as you value the work of others.*

Copyright © 2023 Tam Veilleux. All rights reserved worldwide.

MONDAY, AUGUST 12 – SUNDAY, AUGUST 18

MOONS: SCORPIO, SAGITTARIUS, CAPRICORN, AQUARIUS

Hold onto your panties, Little Pretzel, this week is an astrological doozy. Breathe deep and prepare yourself by resting Monday through Thursday because it all starts on Friday with Mercury shifting zodiac signs. Still retrograde, Mercury will move into Leo providing you the chance to review how you create and express yourself, how dramatic you've been, how playful you are, and how you are showing up on the world stage. Revisiting these topics will provide growth points you can use as you move forward in the rest of 2024 and beyond. Mercury retrograde will last until August 28th, giving you plenty of time to look at your own childlike qualities and review them.

The news of the week is the T-Square forming on Saturday. This event involves hip-to-hip Jupiter and Mars in Gemini, squaring off with Saturn in Pisces, and Venus in Virgo. The astrological event triggers a major battle. Saturn wants us to be disciplined spiritually and creatively. Venus expects us to have high standards in our partnerships now and wants us service oriented while the Jupiter-Mars team is rooting for expansive learning and walking our talk. Do we go inward or act out? Should we stay or do we go? The answer to the T-Square lies in the fiery energy of Sagittarius. As skirmishes arise around Saturday the 17th, truth-telling may be the necessary evil or perhaps a deeper look at your own beliefs before that truth-telling occurs. The T-Square is pointing directly at your own stuck ways and begs for reevaluation. Suffice it to say that the weekend holds much tension. The energy is big. Open-mindedness is your ally.

GIFT & SHADOW THIS WEEK: *This is the week of possibility thinking! It is a "keep your options open" sort of energy. In the shadow, this can be self-doubt or the fear of not knowing. But if we can learn to let the power of possibilities stimulate our imaginations, then ideas become seeds of what more is possible in our lives and experiences. Possibilities are not yet truths though, so we also need to wait until the truth is proven over time. Don't shut down the possibilities because you are afraid they won't become truths. This is truly when open-mindedness is your ally.*

ENERGY ALMANAC CHALLENGE: The T-Square may have been hard on your nerves. What was your experience like? Share it on social media and tag us with @TheEnergyAlmanac so we can commiserate.

♡ Fun, fresh, transformational products + services: https://choosebigchange.com ♡

Copyright © 2023 Tam Veilleux. All rights reserved worldwide.

MONDAY, AUGUST 19 – SUNDAY, AUGUST 25

MOONS: AQUARIUS, PISCES, ARIES, TAURUS

Monday morning arrives and there's still a ton of energy to handle as the aspects of the weekend spill over into it. Plus, there's a Full Moon to contend with. Be sure to read our article on that topic. The tensions are many and varied and you may find your mind racing. Don't let your own drama spill too far into the week. Work with questions. "How can I best surrender to changes?" Or, "What is right about this that I don't yet comprehend?" Tap into your intuition to see what you should really focus on and be mindful of not letting old beliefs keep you trapped in ideas that aren't serving you any longer.

This week there is an ongoing Jupiter-Saturn square. Jupiter in Gemini is gregarious and social. It has you questioning the world while old man Saturn in Pisces is expecting some seriousness about creating your own reality. You may feel in a personal tug of war, confronted by "play with the group" or "stay silent and meditate." We suggest having your cake and eating it, too, with a little of both this week. Book time with friends to have important conversations after you've done some contemplation about your faith.

Venus and Mars begin a square-off midweek, creating yet more imbalance for a few days, this time it's between doing what you said you would and being of service to others. Remember, integrity first.

At the end of this week, your fast moving frontal cortex is registering lots of information about what to do and when to do it. Plans may unfold as to actions you can take when Mercury sextiles Mars. You'll want to take notes, for sure.

It's been a week, Little Pretzel. Rest well on Sunday.

GIFT & SHADOW THIS WEEK: *What are you committed to doing or being? This week we really get to explore what it is that we say yes to and how we enter into our commitments. For some people, saying yes is automatic, and then when they realize they have said yes to too many things they either remain only half-heartedly committed or they have to back out of engagements. Of course this can have a negative impact on our relationships and reputation. Saying yes requires us to use our intuition, body wisdom, or our emotions to guide us to the correct things to say yes to. Then the experience is magical.*

Get your book bonus offers: www.choosebigchange.com/pages/bonus24

Copyright © 2023 Tam Veilleux. All rights reserved worldwide.

August Moons

AUGUST 4, 7:13 AM EDT
NEW MOON AT 12° LEO

CALL FOR BACKUP

Leo brightens up the entire new moon night sky with its fiery, fun-loving nature. What passions can you ignite to light up your life a bit more? Show up authentically for them, because Leo is most vibrant when it's able to fully express itself.

Those big dream seeds are really gaining traction now. No longer are they buried beneath the surface, quietly growing. They're not even tiny baby saplings anymore. They've evolved into recognizable shapes now, so there's no mistaking or hiding them anymore. This makes Leo *thrilled*!

Continue to nurture your growing intentions. But do it in a way that brings other people's attention to them. Whether that's as validation, support, expansion, or even critiques.

Others have fresh points of view for you to borrow. Perhaps there are new opportunities hidden in plain sight you would otherwise miss if someone else hadn't pointed it out. It's time to bring in reinforcements that support your grand vision!

AFFIRMATION: ***"I am surrounded by people who understand, love, and support me unconditionally."***

MONTHLY MOONWORK:

- Call for backup. Attempt to rally like-minded people around you so you can inspire each other spiritually.
- Analyze your daily routines to ensure they're effectively supporting your dream manifestations.
- Practice intense self-love. Look yourself in the eye via a mirror and genuinely say "I love you!"

♡ Fun, fresh, transformational products + services: https://choosebigchange.com ♡

Copyright © 2023 Tam Veilleux. All rights reserved worldwide.

AUGUST 19, 2:26 PM EDT

FULL MOON AT 27° AQUARIUS

RESPONSIBLY FREE

Aquarius is quirky, independent, and easily distracted. Sometimes, it feels nice to take your mind off your goals for a little while. Taking a quick break to rest can reinvigorate excitement. But there's a difference between taking a step back and losing momentum.

Emotional blockages are becoming increasingly infuriating. Aquarius needs the freedom to move, but the energy is sticky. Unstick yourself from heavy emotions by slowing down and sinking into them. They'll dissolve, and it will be easier to express yourself again.

There's so much going on right now. Start paying more attention to things you normally wouldn't. Try seeing things from new perspectives you haven't tried before. Your relationships house endless expansion opportunities.

Today's Aquarius Full Moon is guiding us to strike a balance between freedom and responsibility. Because the two are far from mutually exclusive. What is standing in the way of freedom? What's keeping you from taking responsibility? Again, sit with these now to clear the path for tomorrow.

AFFIRMATION: ***"I am free to rest when I need to. Taking regular breaks supports my success."***

MONTHLY MOONWORK:

- Organize your to-do lists and goals in a way that's flexible, but keeps you accountable.
- Review times in your life when you felt successful. What can you learn from those experiences about your mindset?
- Be more observant while you're out in the world; you might witness miracles!

Get your book bonus offers: www.choosebigchange.com/pages/bonus24

Copyright © 2023 Tam Veilleux. All rights reserved worldwide.

Numerology

The month of August blends the 8 month with the 8 year creating an introspective 7 energy (8 + 8 = 16, 1 + 6 = 7). Last month was a good month to open up and include your circle of family and friends, but this month, you may feel the draw of the 7 energy pulling you to be alone. Don't let that feeling to withdraw lead to a feeling of being all alone. You're not alone, but you do need some time by yourself. This is the time to go within. It's a time to have a chat with yourself and evaluate your thoughts, feelings and needs. Stir up and listen to your intuition, your higher self. You and only you know what is right and best for you. Ask, listen and evaluate. Rest and be comfortable with yourself this month, you'll have time to get back in the mix with others soon enough, for now nature is your ally.

Aromatherapy & Gemstones

AROMAS: TURMERIC & GINGER ZEST Turmeric & Ginger Zest are this month's aromas. They are hot, spicy, bright, and invigorating. They will give you a boost of energy and a new found sense of lightness!

Turmeric is a commonly used spice and is well-known for its healing, anti-inflammatory properties. Let its aroma aid you in feeling uplifted, positive, and soothed.

Ginger is equally as healing and known for its digestive properties. It is important to remember that digestion is not just limited to your gut. Ginger's aroma will also support you in digesting past experiences along with new information.

The energies of August will require that you invigorate your senses and stimulate your spirit. Turmeric & Ginger Zest want you to get back into the healthy flow of your life!

GEMSTONE: PEACH MORGANITE The month of August will ask you to spend time in creative visioning. You are made of infinite potential. Peach Morganite wants you to increase your capacity for playfulness, happiness, and joy. This month, your consistent efforts to stabilize yourself by releasing what feels heavy in your heart will be directly correlated to your ability to feel uplifted, imaginative, and embodied in your high vibrations.

With Peach Morganite, you will put down whatever weight you have been carrying and you will be free to move forward with your new found sense of childlike lightheartedness.

ACCESS THE ENERGIES:

- Diffuse a blend of 3-4 drops of Turmeric & Ginger essential oils or place a few drops of essential oil in your hands. Cup your palms at your face and nose. Breathe deeply to invigorate your senses.
- Place your Peach Morganite in your living room or office desk. Let it activate your creative, lighthearted energies throughout the day.

♡ Fun, fresh, transformational products + services: https://choosebigchange.com ♡

Copyright © 2023 Tam Veilleux. All rights reserved worldwide.

The Tarot card associated with Leo is **Strength**. Strength is a card that represents courage, determination, and inner fortitude. It is a card of resilience, passion, and self-confidence. It encourages us to face our fears, to overcome challenges, and to embrace our personal power. Strength can also suggest a need for patience, compassion, and understanding.

In Leo Season, you are supported in cultivating inner strength, to find courage in the face of adversity, and to embrace your passions and desires with confidence and self-assurance.

STRENGTH AFFIRMATION ***"I am confident, resilient, and patient while navigating life challenges and powerfully supported by my inner strength."***

Merry Meet! The sweet heat of summer is upon us and while we adore basking in the Sun, the warm sultry nights call us. Are you an Astrophile—a lover of stars? A Selenophile—a moon lover? Or both? Under the light of Sirius, the brightest star in the night sky, we are called to settle into ourselves and discover our great secrets. The night entices you into a Star Circle Intention Meditation.

STAR CIRCLE INTENTION MEDITATION

First, create your star circle. Perhaps you will place it in your moon garden. Perhaps, secretly in the open, where only you recognize it. It's a circle where you will fit inside.

Choose 4 rocks. Large or small, they will be your compass points. As the world and all things in it flows in a circle, place your compass points in a circle:

- North, for air, home and security
- South, for fire, passion and creativity
- East, for earth, new beginnings and growth
- West, for water, emotions and movement

Trail salt from each rock to the next, for protection when you are encircled.

When Sirius is high in the night sky, enter your circle. Remember, Earth loves to feel you upon her, connect with bare soles, or skyclad, if you dare! Look up and slowly gaze towards each compass point. Relax into your direction, the direction that aligns with your intention for this magical mediation for this evening.

You may bring enhancers to align with your intentions.

North – stir the air with a Caim, three times, as we did in Litha, to add protection
South – a small candle of white, lit once encircled
East – rock salt
West – a goblet of water

As we are all original and personally magical, find your own words for your intention. Your magic is found in your verse, and not using others' words. Earth in your Star Circle until you feel it is time. You may leave your enhancer, to gather directional energy, to be collected when there is sun. Come back often. Merry Part!

Get your book bonus offers: www.choosebigchange.com/pages/bonus24

Copyright © 2023 Tam Veilleux. All rights reserved worldwide.

Self-care

This is an amazing month to focus on environmental self-care. Your environment is everything that surrounds your body. Keeping this space clean and pleasant can help improve your peace of mind and is an important aspect of your wellbeing. Are there any areas of your environment that you find unpleasant? Maybe your car is a mess, there is a closet full of clutter, or a room in your house that you just don't enjoy. This is the time to tackle it! Look at the bonus page and opt in to the self-care link for a great little guide to help you clean up your act.

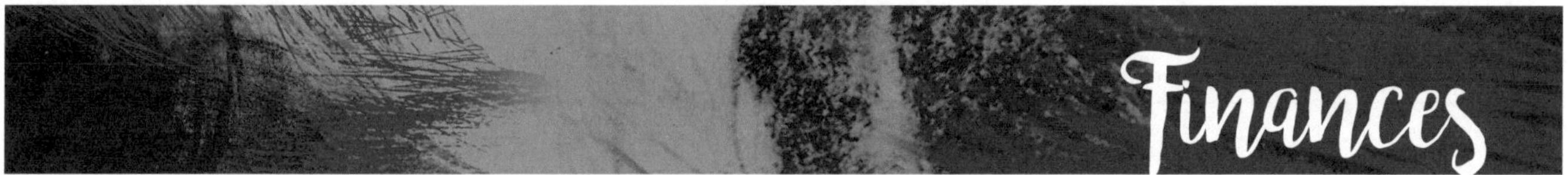

This month let's dig into the comprehension of your old information. Remember how I keep asking questions about your money beliefs? I do that because deep inside of you, patterns have been set. So, as you are redoing the rooms in your home, let's take time to redo and bring order to the environments inside your subconscious by addressing what many call, your money thermostat. It's the amount of money that your subconscious sets for you.

You can check the truth of this by doing a little introspection of what happens each month. Say you have money left over at the end of the month and then out of nowhere your car needs a repair or you get sick and can't bring in as much. These seemingly innocent happenings bring you right back to where your money thermostat is set. It's like you can't get ahead.

Want to change that? Go to the Energy Almanac Bonus Page to get your free You're The One Journal, and find a visualization to RE-SET your money thermostat. I encourage you to do the visualization as often as you can. It will create a repetitive sequence of thoughts that will eventually override your current patterns.

Relax into this and be ok with where you are at, your patterns will eventually change. You've got this!

Holy macaroni, three planets are in retrograde this month and Mercury is going to join them. This is an ideal time to reconnect with our breath by laughing and PLAYING!

Laughter is not about laughing. It is actually about cultivating childlike playfulness. Once you learn to play, you don't have to laugh. Laughter will be the natural outcome of your playful inner child. We have all heard that the average 4-year-old laughs 400 times a day while the average adult laughs an estimated 15 to 20 times a day and when we laugh it is usually because OF something. As we get older, we are taught that something has to be funny in order for us to laugh but that is not the case.

An objective of Laughter Yoga is to cultivate your childlike playfulness. There is a special **Childlike Cheer** that we do whenever we have completed an activity or exercise. To do this activity, you clap your hands and say, "very good," and then clap again and say "very good," and then swing your arms up in a Y shape with the thumbs up in childish exuberance and exhilaration, and say "YAY!" This chanting of "Very good, very good, yay" in between laughter exercises and breathing exercises helps to maintain the energy levels and builds up the enthusiasm.

I recommend that you use this chant when you have completed a seemingly mundane task. Finished loading the dishwasher? "Very good, very good, yay!" Just dusted all the ceiling fans in your house? "Very good, very good, yay!" Whatever and whenever you want to—just do this cheer and all will be okay for the day (or at least the moment).

Copyright © 2023 Tam Veilleux. All rights reserved worldwide.

Notes

☆ Get your book bonus offers: www.choosebigchange.com/pages/bonus24 ☆

Copyright © 2023 Tam Veilleux. All rights reserved worldwide.

September

EXAMINING YOUR WORLD

AUGUST 26 – SEPTEMBER 1

DO be pragmatic in your thinking.
DO NOT avoid deep contemplation.

SEPTEMBER 2 – 8

DO think before you speak.
DO NOT internalize self-doubt.

SEPTEMBER 9 – 15

DO allow time for both work and play.
DO NOT be close-minded.

SEPTEMBER 16 – 22

DO seek peace and compassion for self and others.
DO NOT stay wrapped up in overthinking.

SEPTEMBER 23 – 29

DO nurture your visions and daydreams.
DO NOT avoid review and reflection time.

IT IS SAFE FOR ME TO BRING ORDER TO MY TRANSFORMATION.

SEPTEMBER 2, 9:55 PM EDT

NEW MOON AT 11° VIRGO

TWEAK AND COMPLETE

SEPTEMBER 17, 10:34 PM EDT

FULL MOON LUNAR ECLIPSE AT 25° PISCES

INTUITIVE SUPERPOWERS

Copyright © 2023 Tam Veilleux. All rights reserved worldwide.

September

While four planets take a cosmic nap, you may be noticing the slower pace and lack of momentum. Little Pretzel, enjoy the lag and use your time wisely. As you are harvesting the last of the garden goodies you can be contemplating spirituality, faith, the power of visioning, the shifting economy, and lessons in compassion. It's a lot of assimilating, but there's great value in a deep dive, so don't be afraid to jump into the deep end during the last days of summer. In the meantime, the cosmos are serving up another delight and it isn't a Neapolitan ice cream; it's another Grand Trine to supplement the August events. This time, on September 20th, the Sun, Pluto, and Uranus are playing nicely in the sandbox creating a splendid opportunity for organizing a transformation concerning the economy and groups of people. Innovation is likely involved! Don't expect an immediate comeuppance—results could take time. The autumnal equinox on the 22nd is a perfect day for honoring the waning summer season and greeting autumn with a smile.

The summer won't slip away without some beautiful aspects for you to play with. Look toward the 26th as a nice day for planning your own transformation when Mercury in its home sign of Virgo trines Pluto retrograde in Aquarius. Mark the 30th as a day for bringing balance, beauty, and peace into your world as you apply your amplified intuition.

BOOK BONUSES INCLUDE DISCOUNT CODES, EBOOKS, SPECIAL REPORTS, AUDIO FILES AND SPECIAL OFFERS. TO GET ALL THE GOODIES, GO TO
WWW.CHOOSEBIGCHANGE.COM/PAGES/BONUS24

KEY DATES

Four planets retrograde: Neptune, Pluto, Uranus, Saturn

9/3	**New Moon in Virgo,** read moon article
9/5	**Mars enters Cancer**
9/10	**Mercury enters Virgo**
9/18	**Super Full Moon Lunar Eclipse in Pisces,** read moon article
9/20	**Yod with Sun, Pluto, and Uranus**
9/20	**Grand Trine with Sun, Pluto, and Uranus**
9/22	**Autumnal Equinox**
9/23	**Happy Birthday, Libra**
9/24	**Venus enters Scorpio**
9/27	**Mercury enters Libra**

♡ Fun, fresh, transformational products + services: https://choosebigchange.com ♡

Copyright © 2023 Tam Veilleux. All rights reserved worldwide.

SEPTEMBER PREDICTIONS

MONDAY, AUGUST 26 – SUNDAY, SEPTEMBER 1

MOONS: TAURUS, GEMINI, CANCER, LEO

With August winding down and the littles heading back to their education, we as adults can expect some interesting ideas to surprise us Monday or Tuesday. Venus is still perfecting the way we serve others and Uranus is creating a shift in what we value while Pluto is empowering you in these changes. As the week opens, new insights could arrive that warm your heart and prod you to practical application of the information. On Wednesday, those practical ideas could be challenged by deep day-dreaming or wishful thinking. Also that day, Mercury will station direct in the sign of Leo and you can resume your more creative expressions. When you notice a spark for how to help the greater good on Thursday—and you just may—your pragmatic thinking should help. Stay mindful not to get caught up in thinking about it too much. Action toward change is required.

Reminder—this week Uranus joins three other outer planets in a retrograde journey. With so many luminaries napping, you can count on less external actions and results. This is the time to go inward and reflect. It is the right time for assimilating information about what you've been learning lately. "What's right, right now? How are things changing and how do I need to change to keep in tempo? What should I adjust next?" Write these questions down and use them during your contemplations.

Venus, planet of love and money, enters Libra. Here she wears her sparkly, sequined dress attracting all the right partners. She holds gold in one hand and the scales of justice in the other. Notice a natural urge for balance and partnership in the next few weeks.

GIFT & SHADOW THIS WEEK: *Venus is very active this week in opposition to Neptune. She is perched in a gate (Human Design) that reminds us that love, intimacy, and even our finances must be grounded in reality as we live in a physical world. However, with Neptune in the mix at Gate 25-Spirit we are encouraged to embody our higher selves as well in this physical dimension. We humans are the intersection of spirit and matter; where heaven and Earth meet. Remember this if financial, relationship, or self-worth issues pop up this week.*

MONDAY, SEPTEMBER 2 – SUNDAY, SEPTEMBER 8

MOONS: VIRGO, LIBRA, SCORPIO

September welcomes you with an urge to act, pushing against the urge for visioning. One requires boots on the ground and external communication while the other desires quietude for planning a grand transformation. Under Monday's New Moon in Virgo, which you can read about in our article further along in this month's reading, there is some initiating energy that is practical. Do your best to rein yourself in. Containing your urges will abate any wrong steps. Allow plans to unfold first.

On September 5th, Mars, the planet of action, will slip on the fuzzy bathrobe of homebody Cancer. You may become fiercely protective of those you love and may notice some passive-aggressive behaviors in yourself over the coming weeks. Once again, Little Pretzel—forewarned is forearmed.

Your dramatic expressions about the economy or your own value system could get you in trouble on Friday. Stay alert to your words and think before you speak. On Saturday and Sunday, you could feel the pull between sitting quietly and dreaming about the future or getting productive for the weekend. The choice is yours. Maybe there is room to do both?

GIFT & SHADOW THIS WEEK: *Doubt isn't all bad. Without doubt we wouldn't have inquiry and the search for answers to some of life's biggest questions. Humanity has evolved as a result of the pressure doubt places upon us to answer those questions. The problem with doubt occurs when we internalize it into dogma, opinions, and beliefs as a way to maintain a framework in our lives that makes sense—that keeps us from self-doubt. This week addresses the effect that self-doubt has made in your life. How has it shut down your process of questioning what you believe?*

☆ Get your book bonus offers: www.choosebigchange.com/pages/bonus24 ☆

Copyright © 2023 Tam Veilleux. All rights reserved worldwide.

MONDAY, SEPTEMBER 9 – SUNDAY, SEPTEMBER 15

MOONS: SCORPIO, SAGITTARIUS, CAPRICORN, AQUARIUS

The fading summer brings with it a mid-week that starts some clashing energies. There's an internal faceoff between pragmatic application of getting things done and a huge desire to kick back and socialize. We recommend blocking time for both this week because the struggle is real Wednesday through Friday. Saturday and Sunday look lovely. Venus is in her home sign of Libra and she's working with Jupiter this weekend. It's a perfect time period for holding a party, attending a function, and having a delightful time. Your conversations are likely to have sparks flying and my dear, you're like a magnet to others. Have yourself the best time.

GIFT & SHADOW THIS WEEK: *The shadow of this week deals with another mind-oriented issue: closed vs open-mindedness. With closed-mindedness, we rely on our attachment that answers will come to us in prescribed ways—likely through the intellect. The gift however, reminds us that when we relinquish the mind's insistence on using intellect, magic can happen through epiphanies, aha's, and revelations. In an instant, the solution your mind has been working so hard on formulating breaks through with a solution. The key is to relax the mind and let the magic of the Universe work through you.*

MONDAY, SEPTEMBER 16 – SUNDAY, SEPTEMBER 22

MOONS: PISCES, ARIES, TAURUS, GEMINI

This week's astrological actions don't begin in earnest until Wednesday when your detail-oriented thinking mind gets in the way of your creative visioning. It's a serious matter to be sure! And with the Full Moon Lunar Eclipse in play in the faith-based sign of Pisces, we are guessing the spiritually-edged actions will win. Read about the potentials of this important eclipse in our article further along in this month's reading. (Do that now!!)

In the days following the eclipse, you could really feel the urge to participate more fully in your changing value system or your changing personal economy. Your thoughts may be clouded and confusion may be present concerning your part of the needed changes, so hang in there. Tension and confrontation going on between your ears should be enough to make you sit on your hands. Let's all agree that peaceful transformation is needed and let's not have you martyr yourself doing it. The Grand Trine that the cosmos offers us on Friday is a golden opportunity to be of service to the group transformation. This can involve aligning yourself to self-love and worthiness. As you change, you contribute to the world. As you improve, we all improve. The Grand Trine may present opportunity around money as well as your mood. If finances are an on-going topic of conversation, do reread the powerful articles on money we included in this year's Energy Almanac.

The Autumn Equinox on September 22nd is your opportunity to once again align with natural cycles. Ritualize your experience. Gather. Share harvests. Laugh and love.

GIFT & SHADOW THIS WEEK: *Peace is an inside job. You have heard that at one time or another. This week's energy really brings that message home as the shadow energies of conflict and turbulence surface for us collectively and individually. These energies are the primary source of war and yet that war usually begins in the collective mind where we may be fearful of not having enough resources or other similarly incorrect assumptions. The pathway to peace on the planet resides in the effort that each of us puts into finding peace within ourselves, compassion for ourselves and others, and remembering our common humanity.*

♡ Fun, fresh, transformational products + services: https://choosebigchange.com ♡

Copyright © 2023 Tam Veilleux. All rights reserved worldwide.

MONDAY, SEPTEMBER 23 – SUNDAY, SEPTEMBER 29

MOONS: GEMINI, CANCER, LEO, VIRGO

Mercury is the key planet this week! Mercury is the planet of the lower mind—it concerns itself with communication and analyzing. Monday morning could find you still thinking about balance and the legalities involved with what you're witnessing around world change. On Tuesday, Mercury moves into the secretive sign of Scorpio. Over the next few weeks, you'll have the opportunity to look at the darkest parts of yourself. Your fears may be illuminated. Also on Tuesday, Mercury will trine the planet of revelation perhaps granting you insights as to how you can address concerns around self-worth. Wednesday may be more difficult when the depositor of information, Mercury, goes opposite Neptune. Here you have a stream of consciousness thinking tense against your more creative, idealistic ways. Nothing to do here except stay aware of it. Transformation is top of mind on Thursday. It's a powerful day of digging into the unconscious mind to discover what is in the way of transmuting fear. The work you do on this day can have lasting effects.

Take a couple of breaths Friday, Saturday, and Sunday. There is an urge to stay home and have a group meditation with the family or invite a group of friends over to your space for it. On Sunday, your vitality may be lagging and it's the perfect day to stay close to home and doodle, journal, and meditate. Nurturing your daydreams is encouraged. As mentioned in the Gift & Shadow below, this is a week to love yourself in spite of any baggage. In fact, love yourself because you have baggage and are willing to release it.

GIFT & SHADOW THIS WEEK: *We have arrived at the turning of the seasons, which represents the evolving of our consciousness through the year. We are tasked at this time of the year to begin expressing, in the physical world, the things we have learned about ourselves. How have your experiences thus far created challenges and/or learning experiences? In the process of grounding in the learning and evolution that we have been through, we are urged to remember that we are of Divine nature. We are explorers utilizing the 3D Earthly experience to evolve our consciousness which is primarily of Spirit. This is a week to love yourself fully no matter how well your mind thinks it has done in the year so far.*

FUN, FRESH, TRANSFORMATIONAL COMPANION PRODUCTS TO HELP MAKE 2024 AMAZING ARE AVAILABLE AT:

WWW.CHOOSEBIGCHANGE.COM

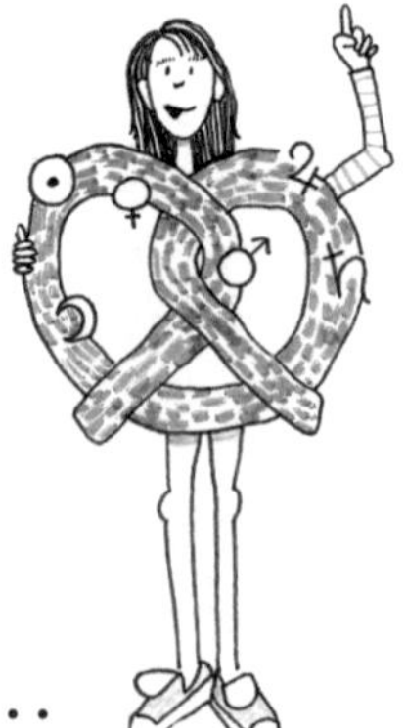

Copyright © 2023 Tam Veilleux. All rights reserved worldwide.

September Moons

SEPTEMBER 2, 9:55 PM EDT
NEW MOON AT 11° VIRGO

TWEAK AND COMPLETE

This New Moon is perfectly timed with the start of the harvest season (Northern Hemisphere). Virgo loves *completion energy*, and we're basking in it now.

All that tender, loving care we've put into our big dream seeds has really paid off. We are finally reaping what we've sown. However, Virgo is already thinking, "Now what?"

Our big dreams are unfolding before our eyes. If we fully embrace it, we can keep the manifesting momentum going. Have you considered what you're going to "do" beyond manifesting your dream life? Other than just living the dream?

New insights are coming up now that are refining your manifesting vision and inspiring you to tweak the process. We're on the cusp of a new manifesting cycle that is being built on the back of the last one.

Most everything we've worked hard to cultivate is still serving us. But there are many things that have run their course. This is a good sign! Now you have more room for *what's coming next.*

AFFIRMATION: ***"The ebbs and flows of life bring me joy! I love exploring new ideas."***

MONTHLY MOONWORK:

- Create an easy to-do list that you can knock out in less than two hours. It will feel *so good* and act like a warm-up to the big tasks.
- Create a list of things that are creating bottlenecks in your manifesting process and potential solutions.
- Take action and celebrate the quick wins!

♡ Fun, fresh, transformational products + services: https://choosebigchange.com ♡

Copyright © 2023 Tam Veilleux. All rights reserved worldwide.

SEPTEMBER 17, 10:34 PM EDT

SUPER FULL MOON PARTIAL LUNAR ECLIPSE AT 25° PISCES

Pisces is dreamy and creative, filled with a lust for life. Normally, Pisces is highly sensitive to energies and prone to overwhelm. That's doubly true today with the intensity of the super full moon lunar eclipse. We're feeling it strongly and deeply, so the opportunities for soul expansion are endless.

Eclipses are a harbinger of new beginnings. While they can be intense, the positive change they bring is exciting. It's time to revise the systems that structure your daily life. Even if it's as simple as rearranging the furniture or trying a new morning routine.

However, Mercury and Saturn are enthusiastic about the changes. As they oppose each other, we'll be feeling far more pessimistic than usual. Make sure this is temporary by keeping hope and passion alive!

Pisces's superpower is *intuition*. Tap into that power every time you catch your inner critic saying something horrible. Ask yourself: "Is that really true? Where is this coming from? How do I let this thought go?"

AFFIRMATION: ***"I am always kind to myself and others. The future is bright!"***

MONTHLY MOONWORK:

- Rest your mind and body as much as you need, unapologetically.
- Stir up the energy of your home by rearranging the furniture or reorganizing any clutter.
- Catch critical thoughts in the act, and let them go in that instant.

✯ Get your book bonus offers: www.choosebigchange.com/pages/bonus24 ✯

Copyright © 2023 Tam Veilleux. All rights reserved worldwide.

Numerology

September carries a 9 energy of completion and transformation and blends with the manifesting 8 year to create a manifesting 8 month (9 + 8 = 17, 1 + 7 = 8). Following your intuition and guidance from your higher self last month, let go of or make changes to things that are not in your best interest. These things that are not in your best interest will weigh you down and hold you back and block what is best for you (what you are working on manifesting). When you release and make changes—it opens the natural flow of the universal energy, the Law of Attraction. The manifesting 8 energy of the year will be amplified this month and you can start seeing some of your goals and projects come to fruition. This is a magnetic energy—when it's flowing right—it will continue to attract and manifest for you.

Aromatherapy & Gemstones

AROMAS: VANILLA GELATO & WAFFLE CONE / APPLE & MULLED SPICES The Autumn Equinox on the 22nd is nature's lesson in letting go. The signs of change are imminent as the leaves turn color and the weather begins to shift.

But before we rush into the next season, let this month's delightfully decadent aromas of Apple & Mulled Spices be a reminder to appreciate the gift of the summer. Let it be an invitation to savor the sweetness of slowing down.

Yes, there is beauty in this season of change and, yes, there is beauty in letting go. But don't be so eager to rush to the next thing. Take a moment to settle in. Savor stillness. Savor sweetness. With Apple & Mulled Spices, find the magic in the present moment.

GEMSTONE: GARNET Let's use the energy of the month where lessons from the past and intuitive downloads for the future come together to plan for a new level of abundance, prosperity, and service to others.

Use Garnet crystals this month as you call on its deep, fiery energy. This deep wine-colored stone represents strength, safety, and self-empowerment. It is important to recognize that when we feel safe, we are able to make choices that are connected to our authentic wellbeing.

Garnet invites you to connect to your inner fire so that you can light up the world around you. Creating a world of abundance and prosperity begins with you.

ACCESS THE ENERGIES:

- Create a stovetop potpourri using apple slices, cinnamon sticks, and baking spices.
- Keep a piece of Garnet nearby during meditation or carry the stone with you in your pocket throughout your day to access your root and sacral chakras.

♡ Fun, fresh, transformational products + services: https://choosebigchange.com ♡

Copyright © 2023 Tam Veilleux. All rights reserved worldwide.

The Tarot card associated with Virgo is **The Hermit**. The Hermit is a card that represents introspection, solitude, and wisdom. It is a card of reflection, spiritual growth, and self-discovery. It encourages us to take time to reflect on our lives, to seek answers within ourselves, and to connect with our inner wisdom. The Hermit can also suggest a need for solitude, detachment, and introspection.

In Virgo season, you may feel the call to take time for yourself, to seek spiritual guidance, and to reflect on your goals and aspirations. You are asked to trust your own inner compass during this time.

THE HERMIT AFFIRMATION ***"I am at ease with my deepest self and use my inner wisdom as it illuminates my path towards growth and healing."***

Merry Meet! As the days move to meet the nights, the equinox is upon us. Light and dark pause briefly together and share time. We have delighted in the abundance of summer, in bountiful busy days. There are dark star-filled nights filled with magic. We now feel the call of change. A sense of something to come, a movement. Mabon, the equinox, signals this shift. A movement towards balance and harmony. Do we need to make room? Clear space for this recasting of energy? Of course we do.

MABON CLEARING

Clearing is movement, a rhythm, a pattern. It stirs the hidden and stale corners. It creates room for new energy. Let us call on the clearing of sound. What sound shall you use? A singing bowl, one that rings with a clear metal tone? A rattle with a cacophony of small sounds that meld together? Perhaps a bell, with a sweet toll. A drum, maraca, tambourine, a flute, even a whistle. Or choose your own hands, clapping.

Begin in your busiest room, the room with the most energy. Send your music up to the corners and down to the crevices as you move clockwise around your room. Are you called to speak? Send out your words to accompany your music. If your room holds an abundance of energy, circle again. Flow seamlessly to your next space. Move rhythmically throughout. Feel the lightness. As the summer fades from your garden, clear leftover energy for next season. Leave your clearing instrument out, perhaps in the Sun, to allow the energies to flow away. Balance and harmony feel amazing. Happy Mabon and merry part!

This month you will notice the wind is shifting into Vata season, the elements of ether and air are getting stronger. You can easily notice this with a chill in the air, frequent windy days, chapped lips, and dryer skin. When these elements affect your mind, you can feel like you are an air head! It's easier to forget what you were doing, where you put your keys, or feel like you are being blown in too many directions. I have a quick video with 10 simple tips to help you stay in balance over the next few months. Go to the self-care section on the bonus page to grab the link to the video.

Copyright © 2023 Tam Veilleux. All rights reserved worldwide.

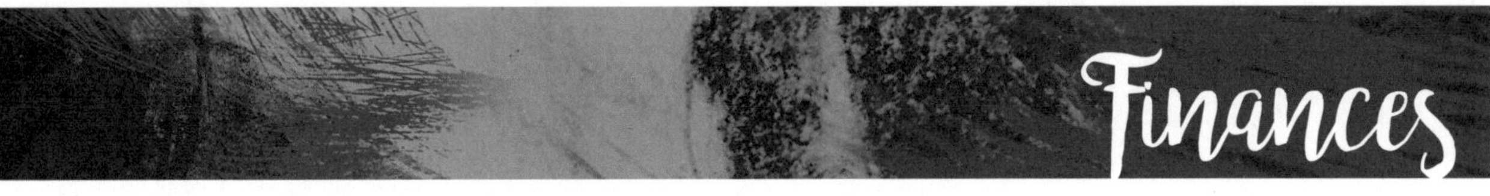

Sometimes a slower pace is what we need. Your Parts surely do. They need time to contemplate the compassion you have for them. You are building compassion for them. It's ok to do the deep dive and meet them where they are at. Accept and love that little 5-year-old Part who wanted something and was told that money doesn't grow on trees. Can you imagine? A little child doesn't know what that means. Is there a Part who did not learn to receive because it wasn't safe to receive? And now, as an adult, it's difficult for you to let in opportunities for receiving?

This month, use your You're The One Journal and dive deep into your own thoughts and dreams of what money means to you and how it can bring balance, beauty and peace into your life. What does that look like for you? Use the following prompts to discover more:

1. Am I ok with receiving?
2. Contemplating spirituality and using the power of visioning, what does money mean to me?
3. How can I be more compassionate for my own and other's money situations?
4. Results take time, can I be ok with that?
5. How can I use money to bring balance and peace into my world?

Summer is ending, fall is creeping in, and the work grind may be back in full swing. If you work full time—whether that's running a household or a business, you are probably quite busy this time of year. And what do we have no time for when we get busy? Ourselves. Dr. William Fry of Stanford University proved that 10 minutes of hearty laughter is equal to 30 minutes on a rowing machine. This is not in terms of muscular movement but of cardiopulmonary endurance. The purpose of aerobic exercise is to stimulate heart rate, increase blood circulation, supply oxygen, and remove waste products. Laughing does all of those things without the cost of a gym membership or the time it takes to get to the gym.

But not all environments are "appropriate" for laughing. That doesn't mean we can't laugh there; it just means that it may be frowned upon. So what do we do when that happens? **Silent Laughter** to the rescue!

Silent Laughter is exactly what it sounds like, we laugh without any sound. Similar to our one-minute laughter challenge from January, try the Silent Laugh for one minute. Oh yes, this may be a good one to do in front of the mirror. Set a timer and then laugh very quietly as if someone is sleeping in the adjoining room and you don't want to wake them up. Open your mouth wide open, and look at yourself while laughing without sound. Or maybe you're on a teleconference call and need a moment to yourself—go ahead and laugh but don't let anyone else hear you!

Don't forget that it takes 10 minutes of hearty laughter to equal 30 minutes of cardio exercise. Can you switch between silent and real laughter and build up to 10 minutes this month? Remember, the more you laugh, the more calories you burn.

Copyright © 2023 Tam Veilleux. All rights reserved worldwide.

✯ Get your book bonus offers: www.choosebigchange.com/pages/bonus24 ✯

Copyright © 2023 Tam Veilleux. All rights reserved worldwide.

October

UNFOLDING POTENTIALS

SEPTEMBER 30 – OCTOBER 6

DO focus on what is working for you.
DO NOT stay in a victim mindset.

OCTOBER 7 – 13

DO be open to adjusting your plans.
DO NOT be afraid to demonstrate your knowledge.

OCTOBER 14 – 20

DO reconnect with your inner wisdom.
DO NOT be fearful of the future.

OCTOBER 21 – 27

DO address the impact of failure-thinking.
DO NOT be afraid to be authentically you.

IT IS SAFE FOR ME TO FACE UNEXPECTED CHANGE.

OCTOBER 2, 2:49 PM EDT

NEW MOON SOLAR ECLIPSE AT 10° LIBRA

IT'S ALL BEAUTIFUL

OCTOBER 17, 7:26 AM EDT

FULL MOON AT 24° ARIES

SOLITUDE SERVES RELATIONSHIPS

♡ Love the Energy Almanac? Tag us on social media: @TheEnergyAlmanac ♡

Copyright © 2023 Tam Veilleux. All rights reserved worldwide.

October

The fresh air of October, always a delight, brings with it big cosmic opportunities starting with yet another Grand Trine. October 5th finds Venus, Saturn, and Mars dancing a jig and creating the chance for incredible insights to land. Information from across the veil is sure to show up and you'll surely feel part of the matrix. Your work? To stay present, make notes, and act accordingly, trusting that it's all unfolding perfectly. The second major transit you want to take note of happens on October 11th. Pluto, who has been working on creating changes Aquarian-style, will station direct, giving you the opportunity to apply any adjustments that you notice need to be made since the retrograde began. You made notes about that, didn't you? Well make notes about this too. There are two astrological yods in October. Yods are typically turning points. They can be surprising and can also create frustration. It's as though there's a force of energy driving the bus and the riders would like to get off, but can't. Not all yods are awful. October 11th has Mercury in Libra, working with Neptune and Uranus both retrograde, and seven days later, on October 18th, the Sun in Libra messes with Neptune and Uranus. Potentials are as yet untold—keep yourself open. Let's see how it unfolds. Always remember that there are forces out of your control unfolding to benefit the world. Enjoy October 26-31 as a gentle time for your spiritual practices and since October already has plenty to talk about, let's add on one more. October 30th presents another Grand Trine—the fourth one in 2024. This event has Neptune, Mars, and Mercury holding hands. A spiritually sound day is at hand, what a way to wrap up the month.

BOOK BONUSES INCLUDE DISCOUNT CODES, EBOOKS, SPECIAL REPORTS, AUDIO FILES AND SPECIAL OFFERS. TO GET ALL THE GOODIES, GO TO WWW.CHOOSEBIGCHANGE.COM/PAGES/BONUS24

KEY DATES

10/2	**New Moon Solar Eclipse in Libra,** read moon article
10/5	**Grand Trine in water signs Venus, Saturn, Mars**
10/9	**Jupiter turns retrograde in Gemini**
10/11	**Pluto stations direct in Capricorn**
10/11	**Yod with Mercury, Neptune, Uranus**
10/14	**Mercury enters Scorpio**
10/17	**Full Moon Penumbral Eclipse in Aries,** read moon article
10/18	**Venus enters Sagittarius**
10/18	**Yod with Sun, Neptune, Uranus**
10/23	**Happy Birthday, Scorpio**
10/30	**Grand Trine in water signs Neptune, Mars, Mercury**

♡ Fun, fresh, transformational products + services: https://choosebigchange.com ♡

Copyright © 2023 Tam Veilleux. All rights reserved worldwide.

OCTOBER PREDICTIONS

MONDAY, SEPTEMBER 30 – SUNDAY, OCTOBER 6	**MOONS:** VIRGO, LIBRA, SCORPIO

Monday and Tuesday this week start off with communications and the analyzing of the topic of fairness and balance. You may be trying to synthesize two ideas. These days also bring a lack of zest. If you still have your sketchbook handy perhaps some down time in a hammock would settle your mind.

Wednesday, October 2nd, is a spectacular New Moon Solar Eclipse. Sara Rae has done an incredible job writing about it in our moon article. Check it out as a robust resource for handling this lunation. Keep in mind that Eclipses present opportunities. As one door opens another closes. Which will it be for you?

As Friday arrives, Venus, still in the sign of Scorpio, will trine the giver of lessons Saturn. In this position they hold hands and encourage a look into the undercarriage of your psyche to see how you might best die to the old you and be reborn again in a more creative and compassionate human. This big inner work makes for a power-filled date night if you have a significant other who likes to go deep. The rest of the weekend may find your mind doing battle. Part passive-aggressive and part peace-keeping you might feel a bit like a fish, flip-flopping on ideas may be the norm when really what's needed is for each side to take a breather. Release all of your critical thinking for the sake of keeping the peace and lean into the energy of Saturday's Grand Trine. The beautiful day brings a sensual and spiritual energy to the fore. It's a great day for coupling and sharing visions as well as doing kundalini work.

GIFT & SHADOW THIS WEEK: *This week begins a 7-week process of releasing fears of False Evidence Appearing Real kind (F.E.A.R.). The first of these is the victim's mind, judgment, and imperfection. The victim mind is a conglomeration of all the judgmental thought patterns humans have developed over the years. Specifically, this week, we are challenged to let go of perfectionism and being overly judging of ourselves and others. When we overcome this challenge, we see that everything is perfect just as it is in this moment or else it would be different. Focus your mind on what is working this week and not what is not working.*

FUN, FRESH, TRANSFORMATIONAL COMPANION PRODUCTS TO HELP MAKE 2024 AMAZING ARE AVAILABLE AT:

WWW.CHOOSEBIGCHANGE.COM

Copyright © 2023 Tam Veilleux. All rights reserved worldwide.

MONDAY, OCTOBER 7 – SUNDAY, OCTOBER 13

MOONS: SAGITTARIUS, CAPRICORN, AQUARIUS

This week holds the beautiful aspect of Venus trine Mars. In layman's terms, the planet of love and money wearing her black hoodie of Scorpio is skipping playfully through the cosmos with her handsome athlete Mars. Venus is teaching us about affection and learning to trust while Mars is currently making you highly sensual. If you have the time for it, book a staycation and a romantic dinner sometime between Monday and Wednesday. Do plan to kanoodle. Other options for the two-day transit include learning to trust, speaking passionately without being passive aggressive, and perhaps building bridges that heal family matters. On Tuesday you can employ some well-balanced conversation delivered in a witty manner to help take the edge off.

Mid-week we may need to be open to adjusting our plans according to new circumstances. There's a bit of astro-soup being stirred up that could create a surprise communication.

From Saturday through the 15th the urge for fairness, love and partnership goes toe-to-toe with some aggressive behaviors meant to support the family unit. You, or perhaps a leader of sorts, have your own ideas concerning balance, but someone isn't in agreement. Let cooler heads prevail. Sunday's hours may hold additional input concerning freedom.

GIFT & SHADOW THIS WEEK: *We face inadequacy as a shadow this week. Inadequacy can propel us into struggling to know more and more before we ever do anything with our gifts and talents. We have forgotten that there is a deep well of wisdom within us just waiting to be brought up to the surface of our waking mind. This is a good week to demonstrate what you know. Dare to face the fear that you're not good enough or don't know enough. One more certification isn't going to make that fear go away, but practicing your knowledge in the real world will.*

♡ Fun, fresh, transformational products + services: https://choosebigchange.com ♡

Copyright © 2023 Tam Veilleux. All rights reserved worldwide.

MONDAY, OCTOBER 14 – SUNDAY, OCTOBER 20

MOONS: PISCES, ARIES, TAURUS, GEMINI

Monday opens with Mars, the action taker, entering the sign of Scorpio. Your passion for generating transformation will be bigger than normal. Your thirst for what's mystical may be consuming and it's a good time to try tarot or table-tipping. Also on Monday, you may be feeling more curious than typical. With the Sun trine Jupiter in Gemini your eye may be on learning something new. Do notice what interests you today as you also handle your feminine desire for sensuality and your masculine urge to "just do it."

Venus is one busy lady this week. On Tuesday, she's wanting Uranus to compromise about some of the changes the budget might need. Watch for overspending or evolving ideas about what you value. Your imagination is bubbling up some interesting ideas.

Wednesday brings a thrilling energy that you will find useful for dreaming about new carnal ways (if you need that kind of thing!) Perhaps you'll lean on your faith to manifest a new partner that is a perfect match to your own erotic ways.

Thursday, Venus changes outfits. She's dropping the dress and donning the t-shirt and backpack of Sagittarius. Through mid-November, your passion for fun and adventure will be on trend and this all comes with an edge of good fortune. Of more importance is the Full Moon in Aries. Read about this lunation in the Moons section.

Lastly for this busy astro week comes an astrological reminder that change is the only constant. There's a multi-planet aspect at play that could throw a curveball. Be ready to return to home plate or advance to third base. The topic? Probably the legal system, but only time will tell. For balance, enjoy closing up the gardens or hosting your final garden party this weekend. It's perfectly aligned for either.

GIFT & SHADOW THIS WEEK: *This week we face the fear of the future. Working with this shadow means we have to face what might be coming even if we don't yet know which way the wind is blowing. This is primarily about instinctual awareness—the intuition and body wisdom for surviving and thriving. Unfortunately, we have given over too much to the mind and have lost that connection. We now see the future with some trepidation or anxiety because we are trying to use the mind to "figure out" what to do. Reconnect with your body's wisdom as it is still there, a ready tool for you to use to determine what the next steps are for you.*

MONDAY, OCTOBER 21 – SUNDAY, OCTOBER 27

MOONS: GEMINI, CANCER, LEO, VIRGO

This week, watch for the urge to participate in the transformation of the group. All eyes are on freedom, innovation, and humanitarianism for Tuesday and Wednesday. Tuesday you may be writing or talking about your ideas and there's a seriously spiritual tone attached. Wednesday you may experience the impetus to act on your sudden insights. Little Pretzel, do be sure you're taking the right steps. This desire to move is present through Friday. Notice thoughts about money and your personal magnetism.

Little Pretzel, Saturday and Sunday are for kanoodling. Mars, still in the sensitive sign of Cancer, is tickling the armpits of Neptune, who is full of love and compassion. During this transit, which will last until month end, stay mindful. Watch for being more combative than normal when having to fight for important ideals.

GIFT & SHADOW THIS WEEK: *We face the fear of failure this week. Or is it the fear of success? Either way, this week we get to address the impact of failure-thinking and success-aversion. Really there is no such thing as failure, or at least not in the sense that we humans allow it to affect us. Instead, failure is really just a blip on the screen telling us that something needs to be tweaked or changed in order to move forward. Sometimes, we get in our own way of success, slowing down the process because we might fear who we would be without the struggle. Yikes—let it all go this week. Do you in spectacular fashion.*

Copyright © 2023 Tam Veilleux. All rights reserved worldwide.

October Moons

OCTOBER 2, 2:49 PM EDT
NEW MOON SOLAR ECLIPSE AT 10° LIBRA

IT'S ALL BEAUTIFUL

Lovely Libra dwells in a world of beauty and bliss. Today's solar eclipse is intensifying the new moon's energy, threatening to throw us off our equilibrium. Maintaining inner harmony is key to bringing the scales back to balance.

This might be a challenge because Venus and Mercury are strongly suggesting we leap outside our comfort zone to try something new. Whatever creative process we've been following could use some fresh ideas. Stay connected to your intentions while also exploring different methods.

We've been busy nurturing the big dream seeds we planted in the first quarter of the year. They've grown from big dream saplings into grand dream trees! Take a step back and admire your phenomenal work.

Manifesting timelines are speeding up now. The people surrounding you are your support group and are a huge part of the Universe's plan to bring you your manifestations. Keep your friends close! And tell them how special they are to you.

AFFIRMATION: *"I am beautiful. I live a beautiful and abundant life."*

MONTHLY MOONWORK:

- Take a few extra moments to romanticize ordinary things in your life, just for the sake of beauty.
- Indulge in all the things you think are the most wonderful and beautiful.
- Do something extra special for someone who means a lot to you within your support group.

♡ Fun, fresh, transformational products + services: https://choosebigchange.com ♡

Copyright © 2023 Tam Veilleux. All rights reserved worldwide.

OCTOBER 17, 7:26 AM EDT

FULL MOON PENUMBRAL ECLIPSE AT 24° ARIES

The Aries full moon is a great time to practice being in solitude. Sometimes people are overly exhausting with their continuous expression of emotions. We're already dealing with our own emotions and mixing in other people's emotions might just be too overwhelming right now.

And while you're enjoying your alone time, plunge into the depths of your subconscious to see what's lurking down there. Venus and Pluto are guiding us far beyond superficial levels of personal growth. Once we're ready, we can take that same deep level of vulnerability into our relationships.

While that may sound ambiguous, it's actually quite practical. Mercury is helping you to communicate directly and clearly, with no confusion. This helps build the solid foundation all relationships need. Even our relationship with ourselves.

Consciously choose patience now. Aries is fiery and inadvertently harsh. Extend kindness to yourself and all you meet. In doing so, everything will work out exactly when it's supposed to.

AFFIRMATION: *"I value my solitude and my relationships equally. I am patient."*

MONTHLY MOONWORK:

- Schedule appointments with yourself and keep them. Use that time for your spiritual self-care.
- Be vulnerable with yourself and with others in order to enrich the quality of your relationships.
- Choose to trust in Divine timing by practicing patience.

Copyright © 2023 Tam Veilleux. All rights reserved worldwide.

Numerology

October's energy feels like a mini new year and repeats the energies of January. It carries the 1 new beginnings energy and blends with the 8 year to create a 9 (1 + 9 = 10, 1 + 0 = 1). You may see the completion of some of your goals and projects this month. You may see some end and start in a new direction, and the rest will be going through some transformations. It's another good time of the year for you to evaluate your goals and projects and make sure they are all still in alignment for your best interest. Let go of those that are not and make changes to any as needed. As always, letting go of the things that no longer serve us opens that path for those things that do serve us.

Aromatherapy & Gemstones

AROMAS: WILD ORANGE & CYPRESS In yoga, there is a phrase "The pose begins when you want to leave it." This message is a reminder to practice staying in discomfort. When the energies of October bring you discomfort—because they certainly will—turn to this month's aromas of Wild Orange & Cypress to give you staying power.

Both aromas are uplifting, energetic, and herbaceous. Both encourage you to lean into your infinite potential. Stay in the discomfort, and see what happens!

The more you practice it today—now—the easier it becomes to endure future discomfort, both physically and emotionally. We cannot always leave discomfort, but through practice, we can teach ourselves that we are capable of moving through it!

GEMSTONE: ARAGONITE Like the stone of Aragonite: You are soft. You are strong. You are everything all at once.

Aragonite is a fairly soft stone with a unique shape like star clusters. The energy of this stone is stabilizing and grounding. This stone is not flashy. It is raw, natural, and earthy. It radiates wholeness.

This month, connect to the grounded energy of Aragonite. It will remind you that you are an unshakable force and that there is nothing you need in order to be complete. You are already complete in the here and now.

ACCESS THE ENERGIES:

- Diffuse a blend of 3-4 drops of Wild Orange & Cypress essential oils during your daily meditation or yoga practices.
- The grounding energies of Aragonite are best accessed while it is in contact with your skin. Keep this gemstone in your pocket or wear a piece of jewelry throughout your day.

Copyright © 2023 Tam Veilleux. All rights reserved worldwide.

The Tarot card associated with Libra is **Justice**. Justice is a card that represents balance, fairness, and truth. It is a card of impartiality, integrity, and accountability. It encourages us to seek truth and justice in all aspects of our lives, to make decisions based on objective reasoning, and to uphold our moral and ethical principles. Justice can also suggest a need for balance, harmony, and equality.

In Libra season, you may be asked to make fair and just decisions, to seek truth and clarity, and to balance the scales in any situation. Staying centered and compassionate will benefit you in this.

JUSTICE AFFIRMATION ***"I am fair to myself and others while taking inspired action in all situations leading me towards greater clarity and fulfillment."***

Merry Meet! There is something in the air, can you feel it? The breath of the earth is charged with new energy. The colorful bright days are followed by chilly, mysterious nights. Samhain is upon us. Do not be alarmed as the veil lifts, for it is not a time for fear. Rather, a time for connection and remembrance. Although Samhain is work often done during the dark hours, it is not dark work. Fear not the tales of wicked witches. For our ethos is a sigh of longing and anamnesis, which is our remembering of things from a previous existence.

Let us create our connections on this Samhain Night. Start here.

SAMHAIN FIRE SMUDGE RITUAL

Create your smudge by gathering herbs:

- White Sage – to channel the changing energy
- Juniper – to invigorate the mind and body
- Lavender – will bring happiness and increase clairvoyance
- Cedar – gathers good intentions
- Rosemary – cleanses your aura
- Pine – to create serenity
- Bay Leaves – promotes abundance

Gather herbs and greens into a loose bundle. Tuck a note of intention for the coming year inside the bundle. Wrap the bundle with twine or string to hold the magic together.

Samhain Fire

Gather your wood, enough to keep your fire bright for the time you have set, then at twilight, strike the match and set your fire. Once the flames are golden, add your Fire Smudge. Sprinkle on some ashes from your Litha Fire, from June, for extra magic. Now, enjoy the blazemoche, which is the tranquility you will have from listening to the crackling of the fire. Find your connections within the flame. Send a smile to the other side. Samhain Abundance. Merry Part!

✯ Get your book bonus offers: www.choosebigchange.com/pages/bonus24 ✯

Copyright © 2023 Tam Veilleux. All rights reserved worldwide.

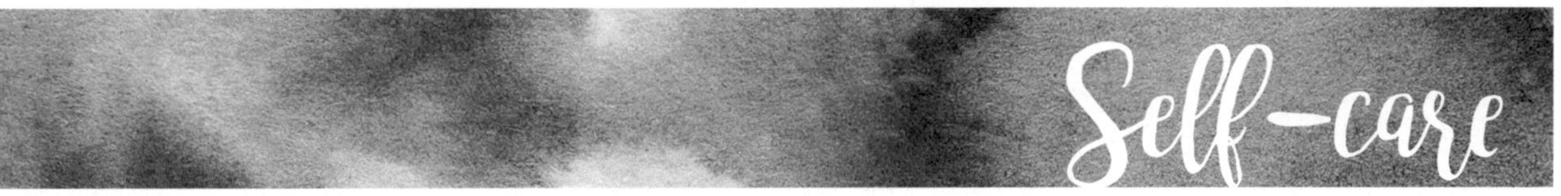

We are officially entering the last quarter of the year. Is 2024 everything you hoped it would be so far? This is the perfect opportunity to reflect and course correct if you want to end the year in a different way than you are heading. As the daylight hours dwindle, our motivation can too! Is there an area of self-care that you have been slacking on? There are eight aspects of wellness in the Ayurvedic wellness wheel that require mindful attention for a well-balanced life. Visit the self-care section on the bonus page for a great guide to help you take stock.

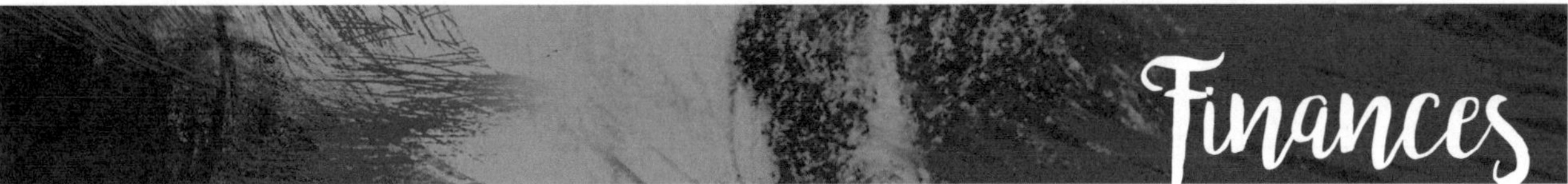

I'm proud of you for taking the deep dive to figure out how to connect with your Parts and clear your money patterns. Now you are more adept at making changes that will enhance you in the long run. Keep growing and let the insights from your own guidance system come through the veil so that you can flow freely with the cosmos. As the energy says so clearly this month: Stay present, make notes and trust that it is all unfolding perfectly.

The subconscious Parts like to feel safe and safe means that they stay the same. But you are doing your best to heal and love your Parts so that they will feel safe enough to accept the changes you want. Use this gentle time to enjoy your spiritual practices as you make changes to your money thoughts and habits.

Some ways to do that are:

- Clear your head so it feels open to the messages coming through the veil.
- Clean your body and gut so it can feel and express its emotions safely and appropriately.
- Get out of anything that makes you cloudy, foggy and feel sad, bad, or depressed. Including relationships that are not enhancing your self-worth.

Need help? Go to the Energy Almanac Bonus Page to get your free, You're The One Journal and learn how you and I can connect deeper and have a private conversation.

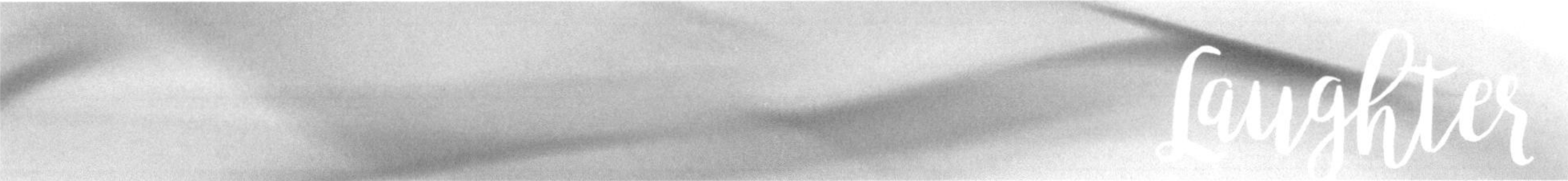

Laughter puts us intensely in the moment and with the month starting with another Grand Trine, we really need to stay present. The ability to fully live and experience the "now" is of utmost importance because it is the only moment where we can experience happiness. People who laugh don't worry as much as people who don't laugh, and as such enjoy life more. Laughter makes their circumstances seem less serious and therefore more tolerable. A playful approach to everyday things is a key factor in keeping healthy. Daily chores are less burdensome when we laugh while doing them. We aren't always having fun, but we do have a lot more fun with laughter than without.

That is why this month, we are focusing on **Regular Activity Laughter**. This is an opportunity to take a basic task and turn it into a laughter activity.

- **Cell Phone Laughter:** Imaginary cell phone "rings," put it to your ear and laugh as though you heard the funniest joke ever. Move around and share with others, laughing. You can also pretend to hold two imaginary phones in both your hands, laughing alternately on each one.
- **Household Chores Laughter:** Keep laughing as you pretend to do household chores like washing dishes, using the vacuum cleaner, cleaning windows and folding clothes, etc.
- **Laughter Cream:** Pretend to squeeze a tube of cream into your hands (or scoop it out of a jar), then apply (to self and to others) and laugh.
- **Make Your Own:** Find something that you do—like making coffee, brushing your teeth, whatever it is and turn it into a laughter exercise.

Copyright © 2023 Tam Veilleux. All rights reserved worldwide.

Notes

☆ Get your book bonus offers: www.choosebigchange.com/pages/bonus24 ☆

Copyright © 2023 Tam Veilleux. All rights reserved worldwide.

November

CONFUSION AND DELUSION, ILLUMINATION AND INSPIRATION

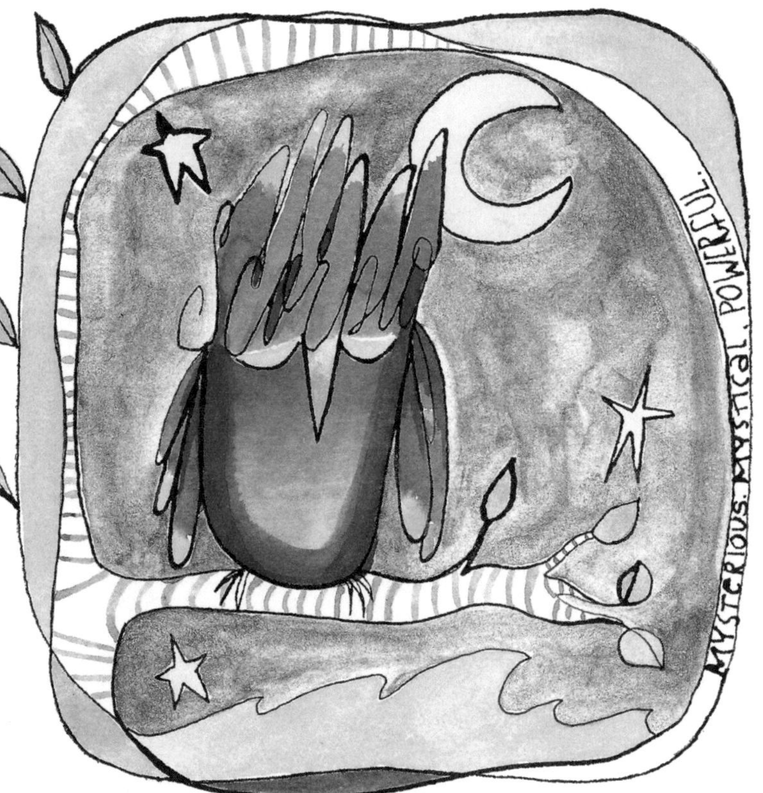

OCTOBER 28 – NOVEMBER 3

DO pay attention to how you're listening.
DO NOT engage in power struggles.

NOVEMBER 4 – 10

DO watch for intuitive downloads.
DO NOT dismiss the value of your purpose.

NOVEMBER 11 – 17

DO block time for addressing the budget.
DO NOT repeat old reactions.

NOVEMBER 18 – 24

DO be disciplined with spiritual practices.
DO NOT over-complicate your world.

NOVEMBER 25 – DECEMBER 1

DO notice your level of or lack of determination.
DO NOT split your focus.

IT IS SAFE FOR ME TO ANTICIPATE BETTER OUTCOMES THAN I CAN IMAGINE.

NOVEMBER 1, 8:47 AM EDT

NEW MOON AT 9° SCORPIO

IMAGINATION AND INTIMACY

NOVEMBER 15, 4:29 PM EST

FULL MOON AT 24° TAURUS

FLEXIBLE DETERMINATION

♡ Love the Energy Almanac? Tag us on social media: @TheEnergyAlmanac ♡

Copyright © 2023 Tam Veilleux. All rights reserved worldwide.

November brings with it an orderly edge. Early in the month, Mars and Mercury, both in the earthy, mutable sign of Virgo, create an advantage for bringing order, and with Pluto and Neptune tagging along, watch as plans for freedom and rebel-with-a-cause innovation, as well as faith are put in place. Later, on the 9th when Venus squares Neptune, you could feel less hopeful about your vision coming to fruition, but it's a good time to work on what you believe. November 17-18's two-day tryst between Sun and Uranus as well as Mercury and Jupiter will bring tension. Again, it's just a couple of days that you'll feel a bit baffled. You want to be optimistic but there are questions that need answers. The two sides need to be examined. Inquiries need to be made. Don't worry much because the November 19th Sun trine Neptune transit will bring relief and some new imaginings. Mercury retrograde, that dastardly little one, has good work to do with you. Employ your analytical mind to your belief system to discover where you have failed to support yourself and why that might be. The retrograde begins on the 26th of November and travels with you through the balance of the month. Lastly, block the 26th and 27th as green days. Green as in—go! The Sun in Sagittarius will skip across the cosmos with Mars in Leo for a playful day alight with hope and expectation.

Here at the Energy Almanac we love November because it kicks off prepping for the year ahead. If you're ready to start loading your calendar, grab the 2025 edition of your favorite predictive astrology book today.

GRAB THE 2025 ENERGY ALMANAC, NOW AVAILABLE AT:
WWW.CHOOSEBIGCHANGE.COM

KEY DATES

11/1	**New Moon in Scorpio,** read moon article
11/3	**Mercury enters Sagittarius**
11/5	**Mars enters Leo**
11/12	**Venus enters Capricorn**
11/15	**Full Moon in Taurus,** read moon article
11/15	**Saturn stations direct in Pisces**
11/21	**Sun sextile Pluto**
11/22	**Happy Birthday, Sagittarius**
11/26	**Mercury retrograde in Sagittarius**

♡ Fun, fresh, transformational products + services: https://choosebigchange.com ♡
Copyright © 2023 Tam Veilleux. All rights reserved worldwide.

NOVEMBER PREDICTIONS

MONDAY, OCTOBER 28 – SUNDAY, NOVEMBER 3

MOONS: VIRGO, LIBRA, SCORPIO, SAGITTARIUS

While Mars and Neptune continue the dance from last month, this week opens with more sexual tension/teasing and a remaining potentially combative nature. Also present on Monday is the internal battle of beliefs and ideals. Let the feeling pass by employing meditation. Midweek finds you tense and scattered as your mind races when Mercury goes opposite Uranus. When the two minds battle you can become weary. Get your body moving to disrupt the rushing thoughts.

As November opens on Friday, there begins a week-long transit between Mars and Pluto. Mars is aggressive and action-oriented, Pluto is powerful and demands regeneration. The two planets in this position can bring forth power struggles. Topics are impassioned. Mars is caring about home life until November 4th before applying itself to creative expression and child-like play; Pluto is all serious business. Watch your words and actions November 1-6. Everyone's point of view is valid and has merit. Don't be reactionary. Employ silence and a steady hand.

Remember that Friday is also the New Moon in Scorpio which you should read about in this month's moon article. It's rather mysterious and you don't want to miss out.

Friday and Saturday in particular will have you contemplating transformation or mystical ideals, you may want to bite your tongue. Timing may be off or someone could get triggered. Though your heart is in the right place, share carefully. Mercury enters the truth-teller sign of Sagittarius on Sunday. Know that the next few weeks may find you more chatty than typical and it will be a great time to plan your next adventure. On Sunday, Venus and Jupiter are creating an opportunity for over-indulgence as well as a potential for a clash in faith. Ask good questions of yourself to find balance. "How can I participate more fully in mindfulness? What is the energy of complete balance? Where can I adjust my beliefs for full benefit?"

GIFT & SHADOW THIS WEEK: *Did you ever play telephone as a kid and pass a message down the line only to discover that the last person has a corrupted version of the original message? That is what we are dealing with this week—corruption. Code corruptions happen all the time in the computer world, and we as people are also susceptible to misreading the information we are receiving. But, when we slow down enough to really hear (and by that I mean listen), then we can ensure the message is pure. This is akin to clarity and is preferable to confusion by misinterpreting what you think you heard.*

Get your book bonus offers: www.choosebigchange.com/pages/bonus24

Copyright © 2023 Tam Veilleux. All rights reserved worldwide.

MONDAY, NOVEMBER 4 – SUNDAY, NOVEMBER 10

MOONS: SAGITTARIUS, CAPRICORN, AQUARIUS, PISCES

Monday morning Mars, the planet of action, enters the playful sign of Leo. Here you begin to notice the energy to express yourself. Perhaps singing or art lessons are in order? How about a course on creative writing? Mars in Leo will have you clamoring to be the star of the show. Read this week's Gift & Shadow section to understand more about expressing yourself creatively. The transit lasts through early January so temper any dramatic outbursts and understand that your time to shine will show itself to you. Have patience and in the meantime practice your tap dance! Ahem. Back to Monday.

Monday's influences include the continuing Mars-Pluto opposition. Remain careful about your interactions because though you may be feeling playful, there is a seriousness to the changing world situation that needs to be addressed. You may notice a softness and desire to set the tone for the week through meditation and solitude. It's a good use of your time.

Watch for intuitive downloads mid to late in the week under the Aquarius and Pisces Moon.

Venus confronts Neptune via a square on Saturday. A desire for heaven on earth and grand ideas about a strong spiritual connection are present. You may experience the energy as an internal emotional battle or as a deep desire to ground it in. We suggest getting outside for a good cry and a loud prayer as a way to abate the sensations. An outdoor adventure would be another good way to stimulate conversation between yourself and Source or yourself and a partner—and what a wonderful way to end the week.

TIP: Mercury is going to station retrograde in December. It's best to start and finish holiday shopping now...as in, this month! Gifts bought during the retrograde could come with issues. If you don't like standing in return lines, shop early.

GIFT & SHADOW THIS WEEK: *This week's gift is in expressing your creative uniqueness. To get to that point though, you must move through all manner of fears surrounding your purpose on this planet. Usually this shows up in one of two ways: 1) an endless search for your purpose or 2) finding your purpose then being afraid to express it. This can keep us in an endless loop of searching for meaning and alternately finding no purpose in existence. On the beautiful high side, when you set aside this fear and just live your passion, purpose takes care of itself and it turns out it fits you like a glove!*

♡ Fun, fresh, transformational products + services: https://choosebigchange.com ♡

Copyright © 2023 Tam Veilleux. All rights reserved worldwide.

MONDAY, NOVEMBER 11 – SUNDAY, NOVEMBER 17

MOONS: PISCES, ARIES, TAURUS, GEMINI

This week begins with Mercury in gregarious Sagittarius squaring against Saturn in the compassionate sign of Pisces. Monday is a great day for journaling your beliefs and then visualizing yourself living them. Employ your spiritual tools that day!

November 12th also sends Venus into the sign of Capricorn where love and partnership becomes more serious and traditional while resources stabilize.

On Friday, another planet finally stations direct, adding to the world's momentum. Saturn, giver of lessons, master of timing, will station direct in Pisces. We'll collectively stop internalizing our spiritual practices but will again engage regularly in activities that amplify our faith, spirituality, compassion, and creativity. Saturn is reminding us that by being diligent and taking our capacity to create our own reality seriously, we truly can make a life we love.

Friday also brings the Full Moon in Taurus, a beauty for releasing old self-worth issues and throwing out old "collectibles" that weigh you down. Read more about the lunation further along in this month's reading.

Enter the weekend knowing you may face an internal battle. Do I take the time for an adventure or should I join forces toward the changing economy or my own self-worth? It's "go on a hike or stay home and use EFT to tap away my worthiness issues." It's "take a class on theology for the afternoon or block time for addressing my home budget." Bleeding into that is your mind calculating exactly how long it would take to bike ride to the beach for a social tête-à-tête with friends. Good luck sorting through it all.

GIFT & SHADOW THIS WEEK: *Have you ever shut down over a fear from the past? If so, this is the week to let it go! The shadow this week recalls patterns in our lives and gives us access to predicting what will happen next. Unfortunately, that cuts us off from exploring possibilities and what could be a new and interesting experience. Instead, if you notice a pattern from your past resurfacing, greet it with openness and watch how you are wanting to react. Stop the reaction, and then respond from a higher perspective. Respect the past, yes, but don't build every experience as if it is on repeat.*

ENERGY ALMANAC CHALLENGE: Share your most helpful spiritual practices for releasing old patterns that no longer serve you. Tag us so we can learn & grow from each other. Our IG account is: @TheEnergyAlmanac.

Copyright © 2023 Tam Veilleux. All rights reserved worldwide.

MONDAY, NOVEMBER 18 – SUNDAY, NOVEMBER 24

MOONS: CANCER, LEO, VIRGO

If you're still trying to figure out exactly what to do next from the weekend's mish-mash of opportunities, you can expect that to seep into Monday. Tuesday brings a deep feeling of love for mankind and (hopefully) great visions, too. Take time on Tuesday to enjoy a good meditation in whatever form that looks like for you.

Also occurring on Tuesday is powerful planet Pluto's entry back into Aquarius. Earlier in the year, Pluto had slid a leg into the silver jumpsuit of future-thinking, freedom loving Aquarius before going retrograde in Capricorn. Now fully stationed direct, Pluto begins, in earnest, a twenty-year jaunt in this sign. Over the next few months, you will start to notice a transformation in how we do humanitarian work, how we use or take our freedom, the way we use AI and other technologies. It's an exciting time to be alive and Pluto in Aquarius will surely prove that out.

Thursday and Friday have some pleasing energy. Watch as someone of authority (is that you?) is triggered or thinks about transformation. Top of mind are humanitarian efforts, unique ideas or inspirations, as well as freedom. You could be downloaded with information that could have effects of that nature. Use your personal capacity for self-discipline to visualize incredible outcomes that impact the whole in positive ways.

Mercury is in its shadow phase this week as he moves toward stationing retrograde. If you're noticing tech snafus or communication gaffs, don't be surprised. Wrap things up now before this planet retrogrades fully next week.

GIFT & SHADOW THIS WEEK: *We might call this week's gift the art of simplification, while the shadow could be named the disaster of complexity! In reality we have built a civilization and our own lives on some very complex ideas, schedules, and patterns. Isn't it time to pare them down and live more simply? Take a look at your life this week from the perspective of complexity. What might you be able to let go of? Are all those unworn shoes in your closest just clogging up the space? If so, simply give some of them away. There are so many ways we can do this in our lives. Share some of your simplification tricks.*

GRAB THE 2025 ENERGY ALMANAC. NOW AVAILABLE AT:

WWW.CHOOSEBIGCHANGE.COM

Buy NOW

Copyright © 2023 Tam Veilleux. All rights reserved worldwide.

MONDAY, NOVEMBER 25 – SUNDAY, DECEMBER 1

MOONS: LIBRA, SCORPIO, SAGITTARIUS

The last week of November is astrologically light. It opens with Mercury, the planet of communication, going retrograde in the adventurous sign of Sagittarius on Monday. Here is your holiday season opportunity to readjust what you believe, end stuck thinking and old routines. If you haven't completed your holiday shopping, do your best to buy things that have no electronic or digital components. Questions for you during this period include: "What do I believe that isn't serving me? What old stories do I keep retelling and why? What experiences have I avoided?"

The urge for creative expression is strong on Tuesday and Wednesday. Make time for doing just that. Sing a song, dance, doodle, draw, paint, or play-act. Be like a child and enjoy the energy for a few hours on each of these two days. Better yet, if you can, sign up for an online course and work on it these two days as a little pre-holiday gift to yourself.

The weekend brings the Sagittarius New Moon. We're hopeful you'll read all about it and expand your thinking as you take on a ritual (see this month's).

GIFT & SHADOW THIS WEEK: *As we move toward the holiday season, this week is an optimal time to determine the level of focus and concentration, or lack thereof, you have in your life. What this week offers is the opportunity to tune into what is most important to you, for example your passion, and not split your focus into too many areas. Fragmentation results and that feeling of ADD or ADHD when we are trying to focus on too many things (and likely not important things). Restore your mind by choosing what is most important to you and turning your focus power there.*

Mercury RETROGRADE

CONSULT YOUR BONUS RETROGRADE REPORT, AVAILABLE AT:

WWW.CHOOSEBIGCHANGE.COM/PAGES/BONUS24

Copyright © 2023 Tam Veilleux. All rights reserved worldwide.

NOVEMBER 1, 8:47 AM EDT

NEW MOON AT 9° SCORPIO

IMAGINATION AND INTIMACY

Scorpio loves mystery, all things dark and sexy. But holding grudges is the opposite of sexy. Deep down, we *really* want to have emotionally intimate relationships. This means we have to be vulnerable and nonjudgmental.

Mercury and Mars are making confident self-expression easy now, which is great for strengthening connections. If we lean too far into this planetary trine, our communication might become overly sharp. Keep the balance and keep the peace.

On a subtle subconscious level, the dynamics of our relationships are being highlighted. It may be hard to pinpoint, so look for clues in arguments, squabbles, and triggers. A power struggle between two people makes it nearly impossible to build trust. Remember, intimacy only grows from vulnerability and non-judgment.

Scorpio loves to delve deep into imagination and intuition. Use this energy to invent, innovate, and *create*. All those intimate conversations are turning out to be quite inspiring. Channel all this magic into creating something unusually magnificent.

AFFIRMATION: ***"I embrace radical acceptance. Intimacy is safe and fulfilling."***

MONTHLY MOONWORK:

- Practice forgiveness to release any anger and tension surrounding old grudges.
- Think at least three times before you speak. Is what you're about to say kind and supportive?
- Embrace the ambient darkness by lighting candles instead of lamps.

♡ Fun, fresh, transformational products + services: https://choosebigchange.com ♡

Copyright © 2023 Tam Veilleux. All rights reserved worldwide.

NOVEMBER 15, 4:28 PM EST

FULL MOON AT 24° TAURUS

Taurus is steadfast and highly successful. It's skilled at empathizing with all perspectives, but rarely veers from its opinion. The Taurus full moon is the ideal time to let go of these stubborn beliefs so we can expand our horizons.

That doesn't mean you lessen your dedication to manifesting your dream life. What this means is being open to alternative paths to getting there. Taurus thrives off plans, but flexibility in planning is equally important for manifesting.

It may appear to be a straight shot to your manifestation at this point. Our big dream seeds are nearly full grown. We've been goal oriented and focused for months and now we're reaping the rewards. That unwavering determination really made a difference!

If you feel like things aren't working out perfectly right now, circle back to stubbornness. What are you stubbornly clinging to that is just dead weight? Are you stuck in tunnel vision? Taurus can easily learn to unstick itself if it chooses.

AFFIRMATION: ***"My hard work always pays off. I am open to new ways of thinking."***

MONTHLY MOONWORK:

- Purposefully explore ideas that are the opposite of yours. You don't have to adopt them, just learn from them.
- Journal about what you refuse to let go of and why you have to keep it. Is it *actually* serving you, or are you just being stubborn?
- Do your planning in pencil instead of a pen so you can stay flexible.

Get your book bonus offers: www.choosebigchange.com/pages/bonus24

Copyright © 2023 Tam Veilleux. All rights reserved worldwide.

Numerology

November rolls in as the year end gets closer and gives us that sprint energy that runners draw upon at the end of their race. The 11 energy blends with the 8 year to create a 1 energy (11 + 8 = 19, 1 + 9 = 10, 1 + 0 = 1). This is that new beginning energy coming around again for the year. This time that new beginning has the advantage of having already begun, then evaluated, then adjusted—so now it is a more focused new beginning. This more focused new beginning energy creates that sprint energy mentioned earlier. It's like your second wind after you get worn out and ready to quit. It shows up and gives you that boost to finish. Use this energy to re-start or just re-focus on your goals and projects that you've been working on this year. Give yourself a little pat on the back for as far as you've gotten this year and how close you are to completion.

Aromatherapy & Gemstones

AROMAS: YLANG YLANG & FRANKINCENSE Ylang Ylang & Frankincense have long been used in ritualistic practices to lift you into transcendence. Bring yourself into a meditative state this November with your smoky, spicy, floral aromatherapy companions Ylang Ylang & Frankincense. You will need them this month to check into your core beliefs and to go out into the world with a clear head. They will support you in staying true to your heart when challenges arise.

Challenges will arise and try to throw you off course this month; they may show up physically or even as monkey-mind thoughts. Before you simply recycle old ideas or repeat old patterns, take a moment with Ylang Ylang & Frankincense. Use it to come back to your center—to realign with your core beliefs. Then, move forward into the world with a clear head while staying true to your heart.

This November, with Ylang Ylang & Frankincense, your mind is clear and you are free to transcend.

GEMSTONE: HERKIMER DIAMONDS As November greets us, you may be seeking clarity and comfort. Turn to Herkimer Diamonds, the stone of attunement, to clear out blockages, toxins, and imbalances. This month, call in and become the energy you seek.

Herkimer Diamonds are crystal clear, shiny, transparent stones. Visually, these gems resemble diamonds as they are a variety of both Clear Quartz and Amethyst Crystals. Energetically, this powerfully positive stone calls in the clarity of Clear Quartz and the calmness of Amethyst. This combination invites you to find a sense of serenity in order to become more of the energy you seek. It asks you to release perfectionism, negativity, or toxic thoughts. It asks that you make decisions that reflect your worth.

It is important to know that what you seek is also seeking you. With Herkimer Diamonds, attune your energy to become more of the energy you seek and watch as all that you desire comes rushing forth to find you.

ACCESS THE ENERGIES:

- Diffuse a blend of 3-4 drops of Ylang Ylang & Frankincense essential oils before or during your daily meditation practice.
- Keep your Herkimer Diamonds nearby during meditation or wear as a piece of jewelry to bring you clarity throughout your day.

♡ Fun, fresh, transformational products + services: https://choosebigchange.com ♡

Copyright © 2023 Tam Veilleux. All rights reserved worldwide.

The Tarot card associated with Scorpio is **Death**. While this card can seem ominous, in truth it represents transformation, change, and rebirth. It is a card of endings, letting go, and releasing old patterns and beliefs. It encourages us to embrace change, to allow things to come to a natural end, and to trust in the cycle of life and death. Death can also suggest a need for healing, surrender, and acceptance.

In Scorpio season, you may be asked to let go of old patterns, to embrace new beginnings, and to trust in the process of transformation and change.

DEATH AFFIRMATION ***"I welcome change as I release all that no longer serves me, and trust as I surrender to the cycles of life."***

Merry Meet! The cold is growing. What is left of the color of fall has turned to brown. The intricateness of nature is revealed. There is beauty in this which should not be overlooked. Here we are, warm in our homes. The darkness slowly creeps in and we turn our lights on earlier each evening. We understand the call to hibernate. It is time to bring Hygge to our daily round. Warmth, connected, restfulness, serenity, comfort, this is Hygge.

HYGGE CANDLE RITUAL

In a place where the nightfall is captured, create your Hygge Alter, perhaps on your dinner table, where it will shine on your family gathering or a window ledge (battery operated candle is best here!) to flicker into the darkness.

A fat white pillar candle will be the center of your Hygge ritual. Place it in a glass holder. Gather around it the symbols of your home and family. Bring pictures, tokens, things that hold the memories of all who are yours. When the golden hour comes, that time between twilight and dark, strike the flame.

Focus on each symbol as the flame flickers and alights. Send all the feelings of Hygge and home to yours. Bring yours over to gather. Sit around and break bread and send a "cheers." Feel peace, for this is the magical end to a Hygge Ritual. As the nights continue to grow, remember to bring true Hygge home. Warmth, connection, restful serenity, comfort, peace. Merry part!

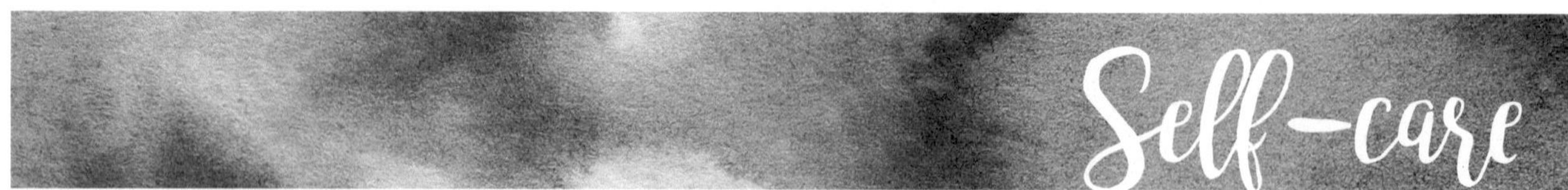

Beliefs are funny things because sometimes we don't even know why we believe something to be true yet we hold onto this belief like it is a fact. Beliefs come from our parents, society, and culture but they are also formed from our traumas too. Your beliefs dictate your life more than you realize. You may not be aware how some of your beliefs are holding you back in life but this is a perfect month to become more mindful of this. If you would like some guidance on how to shift your limiting beliefs into empowering beliefs, there's something special for you in the self-care section on the bonus page!

Copyright © 2023 Tam Veilleux. All rights reserved worldwide.

Finances

The energies this month range from making plans for freedom to feeling the tension of being baffled. Money is a lot like that. One moment it is freely flowing in and another moment it is creating tension in your body. And not always from lack. Lots of people have a free-flowing amount of money, but they end up with other tensions because of it. It's not that just because you have it, it will make you happy. You have to get okay with being happy first, no matter what else is happening around you.

Two things are important here. First, you do have to get your analytical mind on board with discerning what is and is not working for you financially and second, your Parts continually need your help and playful love to feel hopeful.

The inquiry to be made here is, when you feel less hopeful about your vision coming to fruition, to go back inside your subconscious with your Parts and have another conversation. There is relief with new imaginings, so let's revisit another journey to your money stronghold room and get that "Green, as in go!" light aligned and get that money and happy playfulness flowing full on.

Laughter

There are two broad categories of meditation—one is still meditation and the other is dynamic. When we focus on any activity or movement and get involved in that activity fully, that becomes a dynamic meditation, because you are not thinking of any other thought. In this way you start enjoying the activity. Some examples of dynamic meditation are chanting mantras, singing, dancing, playing and laughter. What happens when we combine two forms of dynamic meditation like singing and laughing?

I love singing but I am not very good and while that doesn't stop me, I have learned that laugh/singing is one way I can get around that all together. Since this is usually a month dedicated to gatherings like Thanksgiving, I encourage you to start your own **Laugh/Singing** practice.

Hopefully you know the song, "If You're Happy and You Know It". If you do not know all of the words, no worries—here you go, but instead of saying the words, replace them with ha/he or ho.

If you're happy and you know it clap your hands (clap/clap)
Ha ha ha ha ha ha ha ha ha ha ha (clap/clap)

If you're happy and you know it clap your hands (clap/clap)
Ha ha ha ha ha ha ha ha ha ha ha (clap/clap)

If you're happy and you know it and you really want to show it
Ha ha ha ha ha ha ha ha ha ha ha ha ha ha ha

If you're happy and you know it clap your hands (clap/clap)
Ha ha ha ha ha ha ha ha ha ha ha (clap/clap)

And you can continue on with:

- Stomp your feet – substitute for he he
- Shout hurray – substitute for ho ho
- Do all three – try to do all three ha, he, ho?

While practicing Laugh/Singing we do not have any conscious thought process, and all our senses naturally and effortlessly combine in a moment of harmony to give joy, peace and relaxation.

♡ Fun, fresh, transformational products + services: https://choosebigchange.com ♡

Copyright © 2023 Tam Veilleux. All rights reserved worldwide.

☆ Get your book bonus offers: www.choosebigchange.com/pages/bonus24 ☆

Copyright © 2023 Tam Veilleux. All rights reserved worldwide.

December

REALIGNING YOUR FAITH

DECEMBER 2 – 8

DO simplify, simplify, simplify.
DO NOT avoid your meditation practice.

DECEMBER 9 – 15

DO explore the idea of integrity.
DO NOT forget to buy the 2025 Energy Almanac.

DECEMBER 16 – 22

DO practice embodying love.
DO NOT avoid compromising.

DECEMBER 23 – 29

DO seek solitude as needed.
DO NOT expect others to create your happiness.

DECEMBER 30 – 31

DO read the 2025 Energy Almanac.

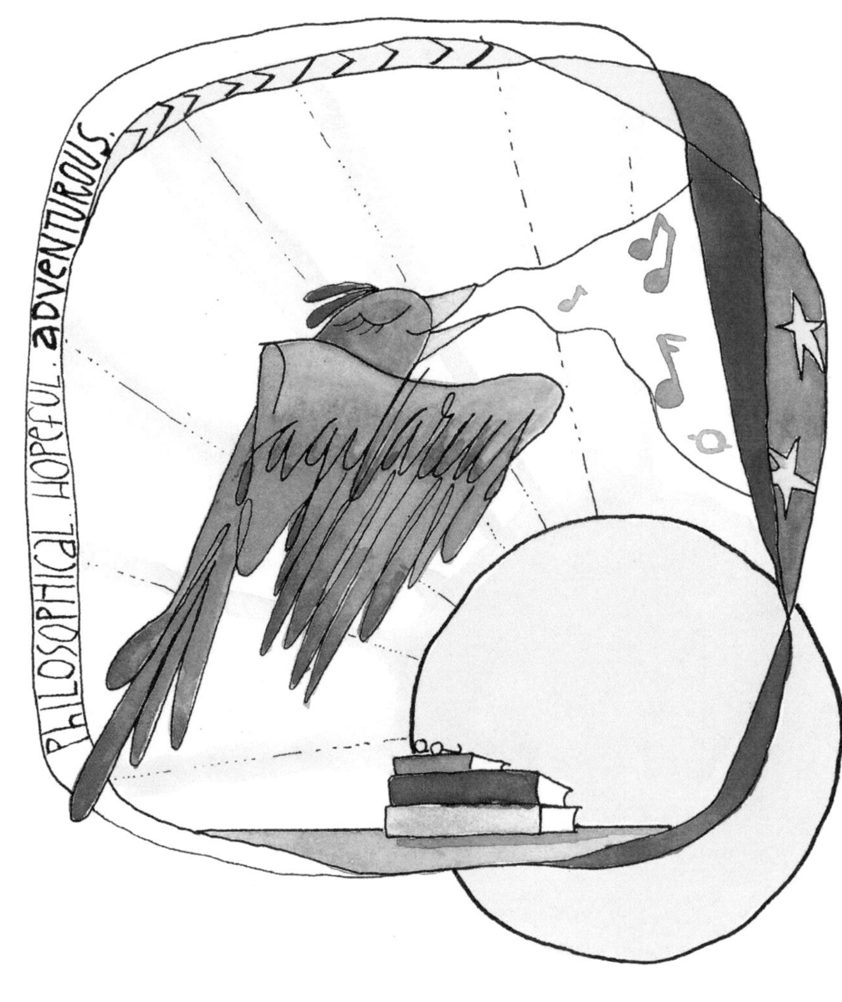

IT'S SAFE FOR ME TO REALIGN MY FAITH.

DECEMBER 1, 1:21 AM EST	DECEMBER 15, 4:02 AM EST	DECEMBER 30, 5:27 PM EST
NEW MOON AT 9° SAGITTARIUS	FULL MOON AT 23° GEMINI	NEW MOON AT 9° CAPRICORN
CALCULATED FAITH	**DISMISS DISTRACTIONS**	**ORGANIZING YOUR DREAMS**

Copyright © 2023 Tam Veilleux. All rights reserved worldwide.

December

December draws us naturally toward contemplation and we enter the month with Mercury firmly retrograde in the sign of the hopeful archer. In Sagittarius, the exploration of your inner landscape is at hand so that you can indeed learn what you truly believe. Your lack of faith or bucketloads of it will become obvious if you ask some good questions of yourself. Important this month is the December 5th T-Square that includes Mercury, Jupiter, and Saturn. The missing piece to this puzzle is the energy of Virgo. This transit forces the need for pragmatism, service to others, and everyday doable deeds. The higher mind is in a quandary and it's time to put pen to paper to work out an orderly plan. Since Mercury will be retrograde during this time period, you may want to continue to ask questions before acting on anything. This planet of communication will station direct mid-month, quickly followed by a couple days of confusion. Of importance in December is Jupiter square Saturn. Here the two planets have opposing ideas and it's time to seek compromise. The topics: learning and compassion (among other things). As 2024 draws to a close, Mars is retrograde in Leo—your creative expression, romance, and desire to play may be dampened. Perhaps you'll end the year in quiet, peaceful prayer.

GRAB THE 2025 ENERGY ALMANAC. NOW AVAILABLE AT:
WWW.CHOOSEBIGCHANGE.COM

KEY DATES

12/1	**New Moon in Sagittarius,** read moon article
12/1-14	**Mercury retrograde in Sagittarius**
12/5	**T-Square with Mercury, Jupiter, Saturn**
12/6	**Mars retrograde in Leo**
12/7	**Neptune stations direct**
12/8	**Venus enters Aquarius**
12/15	**Full Moon in Gemini,** read moon article
12/15	**Mercury stations direct in Sagittarius**
12/20-29	**Jupiter square Saturn**
12/21	**Winter Solstice**
12/21	**Happy Birthday, Capricorn**
12/30	**New Moon in Capricorn,** read moon article
Jan 1-3	**Mars opposite Pluto**
Jan 4-5	**Sun sextile Saturn, Mars opposite Pluto**

♡ Fun, fresh, transformational products + services: https://choosebigchange.com ♡

Copyright © 2023 Tam Veilleux. All rights reserved worldwide.

DECEMBER PREDICTIONS

MONDAY, DECEMBER 2 – SUNDAY, DECEMBER 8

MOONS: SAGITTARIUS, CAPRICORN, AQUARIUS, PISCES

This week is one for the books. Yesterday's New Moon in Sagittarius was sure sparkly and has you in some high-minded thinking. Monday will expand on that energy with the positive energy of Venus trine Uranus. Here we have love and money hand in hand with a changing personal economy. You may draw in unique ideas for using money in ways that please your environment or bring balance to your checkbook.

Wednesday, meditate to expand your faith. Thursday, hold onto your panties, Little Pretzel. The T-Square brings high energy and tension. We are learning to blend our ideas and creativity. Tools for the cosmic event include both pragmatism and faith, practical planning and meditation, doing and being. The square in the sky will require big compassion and a heart for serving others. Lean in, Little Pretzel. Friday, share what you learned about all of it.

Saturday brings Neptune, planet of faith and love, back to the fore. He will station direct in the sign of Pisces. At home in this zodiac sign, Neptune encourages us to deepen our faith, strengthen our creative visualization and love harder. This ongoing transit lasts only through April of 2025 when he begins his 14-year transit through Aries. (More on that in the 2025 Energy Almanac. Have you got yours yet??)

Saturday and Sunday, if you're feeling a tad stymied, the old rock-paper-scissors method of choosing could come in handy. With the Sun opposite the expansive planet Jupiter, the tug-of-war between wanting a personal growth experience or a randy social experience—you'll have to choose. Is it "I" or is it "we"? We're saying, "One, two, three…SHOOT!" And paper covers rock!

PS: On Sunday, Venus enters Aquarius. Imagine Marilyn Monroe in an astronaut's jumpsuit. Here we have money moving toward technology, humanitarian efforts and unique purchases. Here relationships have more tolerance, too. Star Trek, anyone?

GIFT & SHADOW THIS WEEK: *Remember last week's shadow of complexity? Well this week carries on the theme a bit with Uranus the planet of inspiration and lightning fast decisions' move into the Gate of Simplification. I love it! As well, we have another love theme this week helping us to align with what is MOST important in our lives. Part of Uranus's job is to liberate us, and I hope this week you will free yourself from the clutter, the baggage, and the weight of complexity. Keep it simple, sweetie!*

ENERGY ALMANAC CHALLENGE: Publicly share what you learned this year from the Energy Almanac. Tag us so we can thank you. Our IG account is: @TheEnergyAlmanac.

Get your book bonus offers: www.choosebigchange.com/pages/bonus24

Copyright © 2023 Tam Veilleux. All rights reserved worldwide.

MONDAY, DECEMBER 9 – SUNDAY, DECEMBER 15

MOONS: PISCES, ARIES, TAURUS, GEMINI

Thank you cosmos! This second week in December is astro light. Monday through Wednesday, enjoy the moons in compassionate, dreamy Pisces and passionate Aries. Flow with those until Thursday when friendly Venus is opposite Mars (retrograde). This day may find you questioning how you express yourself to the group and at the same time needing to reflect on what is truly of your heart's passion. Friday the 13th, good luck is plentiful when Mercury tickles Venus. It's a great day for conversations about the future. Maybe plan a group date and bring up philanthropic ideas.

The Full Moon in Gemini is this weekend. Don't question its benefit or what you should release. Read our moon article instead. Then, Saturday and Sunday two planets who are retrograde are having some interesting discussions about what they believe and how they express it. Direct the talk if you can. Ask yourself "How can I best express my beliefs now?" Allow the answers to come from within.

Luckily, Mercury stations direct in Sagittarius on Sunday, bringing optimism to communication as we head into the holidays.

GIFT & SHADOW THIS WEEK: *This week we have an opportunity to explore the art of integrity. And really it is an art. We all seem to have a definition of integrity that is strictly moralistic and is dictated to us from society. However, there are other forms of integrity that are very important too. For example, integrity to self or being true to your purpose. Integrity really is in the eyes of the beholder. Your truth is your truth and cannot be downloaded to you by others. Simply align yourself to your truth and values, and integrity becomes easy.*

GRAB THE 2025 ENERGY ALMANAC. NOW AVAILABLE AT:
WWW.CHOOSEBIGCHANGE.COM

Copyright © 2023 Tam Veilleux. All rights reserved worldwide.

MONDAY, DECEMBER 16 – SUNDAY, DECEMBER 22

MOONS: CANCER, LEO, VIRGO

Ahhh, yesterday Mercury stationed direct and we begin to stabilize our thoughts and communications again. Of course, Little Pretzel, you aren't out of the woods. Do let the retroshade period close before taking too many actions. Wait at least one more week.

Monday if you have the time, try cocooning. Nurture yourself as a distraction to any racing thoughts. Wednesday, when the Sun squares Neptune, your imagination may run wild. Visions are big and you can identify with them. This is a two day transit that includes Thursday's friendly and hopeful energy. You can see both sides of the vision and feel hopeful about the future. Capture your thoughts in a journal, and while you're at it, invest in a new journal for 2025. How very Venus in Aquarius of you.

Friday starts a nine-day transit to carry us toward the end of this remarkable year. It's a powerful square between Jupiter and Saturn. Jupiter, the cosmic cheerleader, is wearing the color-blocked shirt of student Gemini. Here curiosity is expanded and learning is top of mind. Saturn is the cosmic lesson-giver. Like a grandfather in the corner of the room controlling discipline and timing, he currently is wearing the artist smock of Pisces where it encourages us to practice compassion and our spiritual tasks. When these two square off, there's a restlessness. Jupiter is saying "Hey, let's take an adventure and learn what we can about education, and let's do it as a group!" while Saturn is on the other end of the line saying, "Hold your horses—silence, meditation, and visualizing your outcomes will bring you further. A patient approach is always better." For the nine days starting Friday this tension will be present. Compromise is needed and there is room for both needs to be satisfied. Do your best to make time for socializing, asking questions, understanding more about learning processes as well as remaining disciplined about using a faithful approach and creating and ending your desire. Make a sticky note reminder for your home: "Inner landscape then outer landscape." Hopefully this will help you traverse this transit.

Saturday is the changing of the season. Winter Solstice is a beautiful opportunity for a reverent ritual. Create your own or use one from the 2024 Energy Almanac.

GIFT & SHADOW THIS WEEK: *We are again at the turning of the seasons, which brings us an opportunity to embody more and more love into our lives. This time it is self-love and compassion for our fellow human beings that is in focus. In the lower expression or shadow of these energies we forget how loveable, worthy, and valuable we all are. Do a self-love inventory. Have you been making decisions in favor of you or against you? When it comes to loving compassion for your fellow humans, are you turning a blind eye to the plight of those less fortunate or do you pitch in and help where you can. Acts of love are favored this week.*

Copyright © 2023 Tam Veilleux. All rights reserved worldwide.

MONDAY, DECEMBER 23 – SUNDAY, DECEMBER 29

MOONS: LIBRA, SCORPIO, SAGITTARIUS

It's Monday the 23rd of December and the holidays are officially here for many. Happy Christmas from the crew at the Energy Almanac! The Week opens with a reminder for you to keep your awareness on the tug of war between being social or being in solitude. There's really nothing exceptional to do besides being awake to it. It's a big energy tugging at your heart. Make your choices and move on, enjoying food treats and sweet gifts, family smiles, jolts of laughter. (Do read our last 2024 laughter article.) The day after Christmas brings Mercury, still in Sag, opposite Jupiter. This brings a chance for you to communicate a compromise. Your beliefs, stuck or not stuck, are at play and you may need to sort through if you are holding onto old information. Keep asking questions through Friday. "What old information is ready to be released?" Then give yourself a good old cleansing ritual. Good tools for this time period include meditation to quell the racing thoughts.

On Saturday, allow in new insights from Uranus who is tugging at you to adjust your self-worth and changing personal resources.

GIFT & SHADOW THIS WEEK: *This Christmas week we can struggle with joy and peace. It's such a hectic time for most people, and then for others there is an absence perhaps of family and festivities. Joy is an inside job as it does not originate outside of us as we think it does. Instead it comes as an alignment to what makes us happy. Your alignment with happiness (and peace) exudes to others in your world. We cannot make others happy or give others joy, but we can certainly set the stage for them to experience it for themselves. Your actions have impact, but so do your attitudes. Let your Joy and Peace be as breath to you.*

MONDAY, DECEMBER 30 – SUNDAY, JANUARY 5

MOONS: CAPRICORN, AQUARIUS, PISCES

The last two days of 2024 are here and the cosmos have no wind left in them except the December 30th New Moon in Capricorn. You are being offered the opportunity to build a foundation under the next thirty days which can support you in a beautiful year ahead. Tuesday the 31st, New Year's Eve, is your opportunity to relax and enjoy as Wednesday the slate is clean, well, except for that little Mars-Pluto arm wrestling that's going on. But, to understand that, do pick up the 2025 Energy Almanac. It's all new and packed with incredible value to guide the year ahead.

The new year is one of deep connection and fulfillment. January 1-5 you may feel ready to make progress in your spiritual practices as you also sense the urgency to act on needed transformation. We encourage your full participation in humanitarian efforts, innovation, rebel-with-a-cause behaviors and new ways with freedom.

You are the change the world needs. Thank you for your full participation. See you in the new year.

GIFT & SHADOW THIS WEEK: *As we end one year and begin another, look back with eyes wide open. What were your successes this year? What do you feel you have left undone or would like to complete? This is a great week to inventory and do some introspection. However, it's not a time to shame, blame, or guilt-trip yourself for what you didn't accomplish. Use those things as a launching pad for what comes next in this new year. Ask yourself questions like, "What more is possible?" You can end this year on a positive note and set yourself up for a beautiful 2025 with that single question.*

♡ Fun, fresh, transformational products + services: https://choosebigchange.com ♡

Copyright © 2023 Tam Veilleux. All rights reserved worldwide.

December Moons

DECEMBER 1, 1:21 AM EST
NEW MOON AT 9° SAGITTARIUS

CALCULATED FAITH

The new moon in Sagittarius has us feeling more capable than we ever have felt before. Because of all the incredible moon manifesting work we've done throughout 2024, we're in a unique position than we were before.

Sagittarius brings out the most bubbly parts of our personalities. We're dripping in positivity and optimism now. This makes it the perfect time to consider what next year's big dream seeds will hold!

What is it you truly value? Freedom? Outdoors? Expression? Honesty? Whatever is non-negotiable for you should be at the heart of all your decisions, dreams, intentions, and relationships. Never sacrifice your values for the sake of fake positivity or fake support.

Sagittarius is notorious for taking leaps of faith. But the thing is, you've been perched on the edge of that leap for a *long time*. It's probably not nearly as scary as you've convinced yourself it is. And there's only one way to find out!

AFFIRMATION: ***"I trust myself and the Universe. I choose to be optimistic as well as discerning."***

MONTHLY MOONWORK:

- Broaden your mind by learning a new subject or a new skill.
- Write your values in your journal, and get in the habit of consulting them whenever it's time to act or make decisions.
- Take that leap! You're more than ready.

Copyright © 2023 Tam Veilleux. All rights reserved worldwide.

DECEMBER 15, 4:02 AM EST

FULL MOON AT 23° GEMINI

DISMISS DISTRACTIONS

The dual mind of Gemini brings us lots of things, including the temptation to change our minds too often. This Gemini full moon is challenging us to find a balance between the two extremes of being "all in" and "something new."

Last month, the moon guided us to take a leap of faith. This month, we're being guided to *continue* down that path, despite the temptation to go in another direction. However, there's a difference between "shiny object syndrome" (where we get easily distracted) and being intuitively *led*.

Do you have a history of leaving projects unfinished? If so, think twice about changing directions right now. Does the potential alternative path resonate with your soul in a way you can't really explain rationally? If so, this could be the Universe's way of helping you manifest greatness.

Uranus is helping us detach from society right now, which is excellent for intuitive discernment. And with Mercury retrograde ending, we can begin learning *new* things instead of reviewing what we've already learned.

AFFIRMATION: ***"My intuition is strong and speaks to me clearly. I trust my intuition."***

MONTHLY MOONWORK:

- Prioritize meditating in solitude because that's the best way to tap into your intuition.
- Take inventory of your current open projects, and decide what to scrap and what to complete. Make a plan and stick to it.
- Review all you've learned this month and implement it wisely.

♡ Fun, fresh, transformational products + services: https://choosebigchange.com ♡

Copyright © 2023 Tam Veilleux. All rights reserved worldwide.

DECEMBER 30, 5:27 PM EST

NEW MOON AT 9° CAPRICORN

ORGANIZING YOUR DREAMS

Surprise! A bonus new moon for you this month, aptly nicknamed a Black Moon. With the new calendar year mere hours away, we're probably already brimming with "new year, new me" energy.

The new moon earlier this month had us inspired to take a leap of faith. And now that we've landed, Capricorn is here to keep the momentum going. You're going to be making all the to-do lists and buttoning up all the projects this week.

Don't skip this important admin work, you don't want to be taking anything unfinished into the new year. Tasks that help you stay organized and support your big dreams are the highest priority for Capricorn.

Flip back to the first pages of this book. Honor the version of yourself that wrote those words twelve months ago. You started at base camp, and spent the whole year climbing the mountain.

As 2024 comes to a close, I want to encourage you to *look back down the mountain.* And thank yourself for committing to your spiritual expansion. Also thank you, for coming on this Lunar journey with me!

AFFIRMATION: ***"I love doing the spiritual work I'm called to do! I easily manifest everything I want and need."***

MONTHLY MOONWORK:

- Brain dump, again! As much as you need. Make all the lists, write out all the plans. Get it out of your brain so you can think more clearly.
- Button up nearly finished projects. Cross T's and dot I's so you can start 2025 with a clean slate.
- Look back down the mountain, and honor the progress you've made in 2024.

☆ Get your book bonus offers: www.choosebigchange.com/pages/bonus24 ☆

Copyright © 2023 Tam Veilleux. All rights reserved worldwide.

Numerology

What a nice energy to finish off the year and wrap up your goals and projects that you've been working on all year. December's 3 energy blends with the 8 year to create a balanced and stable 2 energy (12 + 8 = 20, 2 + 0 = 2). This is a good energy to enjoy how far you've come and enjoy the projects and goals that you have completed. You may not feel a busy energy that drives activity this month, it'll feel more about enjoying the work that has already been completed. The 2 energy is about partnerships, so don't spend the month alone enjoying the rewards of your work. Share it with your family, friends, partner or team. If they assisted and supported you along the way, celebrate with them and let them celebrate your accomplishments.

Aromatherapy & Gemstones

AROMAS: DARK ROSE & PATCHOULI The energies of the month may have us feeling rigid as the year comes to a close. Amidst all of your planning, remember to schedule in time for stillness to tune into your heart and practice self-compassion. December's aromas, Dark Rose & Patchouli are your invitation to give yourself the gift of self-love and compassion.

Dark Rose is sweet and floral. It is effortlessly and inherently the fragrance of love. Patchouli's sweet fragrance is equally as sweet and intoxicating. It is also symbolic of and known for its loving and passionate qualities.

At the heart of love is compassion. With the support of Dark Rose & Patchouli, make it a daily practice to take the time you need to tend to your own heart. Begin in stillness with compassion for yourself. Give yourself the gift of self-love and compassion so that you may extend your love to others.

GEMSTONE: OBSIDIAN During the month of December there are a lot of energies at play that may feel destabilizing. With Obsidian's grounding properties, you will be able to open your mind and spirit to all that the month has to offer you regardless of what is going on in the world around you.

Obsidian's deep black coloring is intense, direct and incredibly protective. Use this grounding energy to find comfort and feel safe within your mind, body, and nervous system. It will allow you to take what resonates with you and let go of the rest. As long as you are open to shifts taking place, everything will happen just as it is meant to.

ACCESS THE ENERGIES:

- Diffuse a blend of 3-4 drops of Rose & Patchouli essential oils before or during your daily meditation practice.
- Keep your Obsidian nearby during meditation or wear as a piece of jewelry to protect your energy throughout your day and ward off negativity.

♡ Fun, fresh, transformational products + services: https://choosebigchange.com ♡

Copyright © 2023 Tam Veilleux. All rights reserved worldwide.

The Tarot card associated with Sagittarius is **Temperance.** Temperance is a card that represents balance, harmony, and moderation. It is a card of healing, self-control, and inner peace. It encourages us to find balance in our lives, to approach things with a calm and patient mindset, and to find a middle ground in any situation. Temperance can also suggest a need for self-care, self-discipline, and patience.

In Sagittarius season, you may feel a need to find balance in your life, to take a moderate and thoughtful approach to any situation, and to practice self-control and patience in pursuit of your goals.

TEMPERANCE AFFIRMATION ***"I am at peace and patient with myself and others as I heal, grow and achieve my goals."***

Merry Meet!
Here we are my friends, at the end of a magical year and a new one soon to begin. On the eve of the shortest day and the longest of nights, call forth blessings for you and all you love, all of yours!

WINTER SOLSTICE

This winter eve, may we all gather close,
To flame the candles and feel the warmth.

To light the way and spare the dark,
Our hopes shine, our love spark.

As the Sun grows and bright regains,
Embrace and echo all again.

Thankful peace and joy abounds
Here and now, it is all found.

All this we share and know
This and every year, as we go.

Until we meet again,
Lady Kara

✯ Get your book bonus offers: www.choosebigchange.com/pages/bonus24 ✯

Copyright © 2023 Tam Veilleux. All rights reserved worldwide.

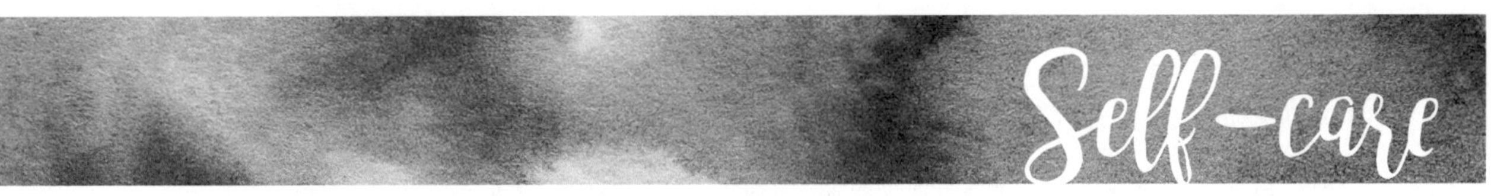

Kapha season is here and reminds us that nothing in nature blooms year round. Since the invention of electricity, we no longer have to follow nature's cycles even though we actually should. We are part of nature, not separate from it. Kapha is a combination of earth and water, put those together and you get mud. This heavier energy in the environment can show up in your body and mind as feeling lethargic, wanting to isolate and withdraw, having excess mucus and congestion, gaining weight, food cravings, oily skin, and depression. I know you may be craving those heavy, comforting foods but it will only feed the imbalance. Go to the bonus page to learn how to thrive in the winter!

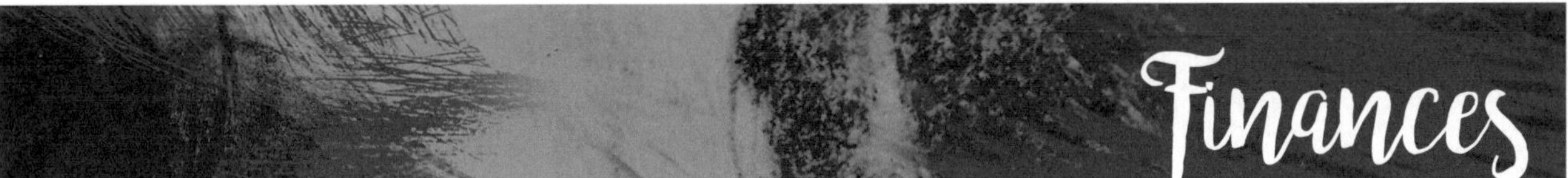

This month remember to use contemplation and exploration of your inner landscape/Parts to learn what is important to you in all things, especially money.

If you haven't set up a time to go over a financial plan, this would be a great month to do that. The energies offer you learning, compassion and ask you to put pen to paper and work out an orderly plan. Getting a free financial needs analysis so that you know your financial independence number and can build a strong financial house is definitely part of an orderly plan.

As for your Parts, oh they love you so much for learning how to connect with them. Keep checking in to see what they need, especially in a busy holiday season. And especially this month because some of the energies are going to dampen things and you will need to compromise at times.

This is the perfect time to ask questions before acting on your money spending. Do I need this, or do I want this? Is it necessary? Am I setting myself up for success? Things of that nature. Just keep checking in with your Parts. Love and care for them like you want to be loved and cared for. Eventually you will align as you end the year in quiet, peaceful prayer.

The days are getting longer, the end of the year is upon us, and stress may be creeping up. But guess what? Because we have been practicing Laughter Yoga for eleven months, we have learned that we get to choose how and when we laugh. Play is real. Serious is fake. Laughter Yoga is a path of spontaneous self-liberation. We want spontaneous laughter, so we force it, simulate it, fake it until we make it. Laugh until we cry or cry until we laugh. This is called the Flip Flop Principle.

Now I will walk you through **Laugh and Cry Laughter**. When you laugh, your body is both shutting down the release of stress hormones and releasing feel-good endorphins. When you cry, your body is reacting to intense emotions and the fight-or-flight response kicks in. To vacillate or flip/flop between the two is an exercise in playfulness.

Start laughing—once you have laughed for 15-30 seconds, switch to fake crying, then switch back. Do this for about 5 minutes to see how quickly you can change from laughing to crying. It may be hard, but resist the temptation to hold back tears. When you cry, your brain releases endorphins, which act like pain relievers to boost your mood.

What a way to end the year—with self-liberation! Understanding the connection between laughing and crying and knowing that we have the ability to change the energy in our bodies in a mere matter of seconds is incredible. I hope you have found these laughter exercises helpful and I hope you continue to laugh well into 2025 and beyond!

Copyright © 2023 Tam Veilleux. All rights reserved worldwide.

DO YOU WANT TO KNOW

What 2025 Will Bring?

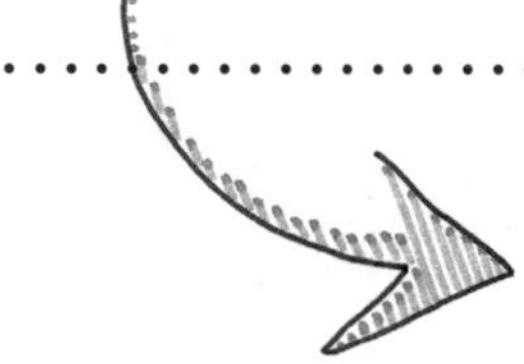

ORDER THE NEW

Energy Almanac

ENERGY ALMANAC FOR 2025, TODAY!

Go to: **https://choosebigchange.com**

GET OTHER INCREDIBLE PRODUCTS TO MAKE YOUR TRANSFORMATION FAST, FUN, AND EASY!

https://choosebigchange.com

Copyright © 2023 Tam Veilleux. All rights reserved worldwide.

♡ Love the Energy Almanac? Tag us on social media: @TheEnergyAlmanac ♡
Copyright © 2023 Tam Veilleux. All rights reserved worldwide.

Notes

Copyright © 2023 Tam Veilleux. All rights reserved worldwide.

Made in United States
Troutdale, OR
12/18/2023

16113732R00102